HOW ONE MAN CHANGED THE WORLD WITH A PAIR OF SCISSORS

VIDAL SASSOON

RIZZOLI
NEW YORK

New York Paris London Milan

FIRST PUBLISHED IN THE UNITED STATES OF AMERICA IN 2012
BY RIZZOLI INTERNATIONAL PUBLICATIONS, INC.
300 PARK AVENUE SOUTH
NEW YORK, NY 10010
WWW.RIZZOLIUSA.COM

2012 2013 2014 2015 / 10 9 8 7 6 5 4 3 2 1

DISTRIBUTED IN THE U.S. TRADE BY RANDOM HOUSE, NEW YORK

PRINTED IN CHINA

ISBN: 978-0-8478-3859-2

LIBRARY OF CONGRESS CATALOG CONTROL NUMBER: 2012934213

VIDAL SASSOON IS A LIVING LEGEND.

HE CREATED A REVOLUTION, A WHOLE NEW FREEDOM FOR WOMEN. I THINK IT'S A STYLE, A CUT, AN APPROACH TO HAIR THAT TRULY REVOLUTIONIZED NOT JUST HAIR BUT FASHION AND SO MANY THINGS. YOU COULD BE UPSIDE-DOWN AND YOUR HAIR STILL LOOKED PERFECT. IT WAS FUN.

HE GAVE ME THE OPPORTUNITY. HE PUT ME THERE. SHOOTS WERE DIFFERENT IN THOSE DAYS. IT WAS JUST THE MODEL AND THE PHOTOGRAPHER. NOBODY ON SET DOING HAIR, SO IF YOU ARRIVED WITH THE CUT OF THE MOMENT, YOU WERE SOUGHT AFTER. I WAS LUCKY.

GRACE CODDINGTON

AS COUTURIERS, DESIGNERS AND PHOTOGRAPHERS SUCH AS BAILEY AND DONOVAN SAID TO ME, "VIDAL SASSOON INVENTED THE WAY YOU LOOK MARY—YOU HAVE THE MODERN FACE BECAUSE VIDAL SASSOON INVENTED IT." **MARY QUANT**

VIDAL SASSOON
HOW ONE MAN CHANGED THE WORLD WITH A PAIR OF SCISSORS
BY MICHAEL GORDON

VIDAL SASSOON PASSED AWAY ON MAY 9TH, 2012. HE HAD BEEN FIGHTING LEUKEMIA FOR A NUMBER OF YEARS, YET IN HIS TYPICAL WAY YOU WOULD NEVER KNOW IT. WE HAD NOT SEEN EACH OTHER IN A FEW MONTHS AND I FELT THE NEED TO VISIT HIM, I WAS FORTUNATE TO HAVE SPENT THE WEEKEND WITH HIM SHORTLY BEFORE HE PASSED AWAY. WHEN WE WERE SITTING ALONE HE SAID, "YOU KNOW I HAVE TRIED TO LIVE MY LIFE WITH DIGNITY, AND I WOULD LIKE TO DIE WITH DIGNITY," WHICH I THINK HE DID. HIS WONDERFUL AND ATTENTIVE WIFE RONNIE DRESSED HIM IN HIS SAVILE ROW PAJAMAS AND DOUGIE HAYWARD DRESSING GOWN AND EXPLAINED TO THE MORTICIAN THAT HE WAS NOT TO BE UNDRESSED RATHER HE WANTED THIS TO BE HIS FINAL CLOTHING. THIS GIVES YOU A BIT OF INSIGHT INTO THE KIND OF PERSON VIDAL WAS. I THINK WHAT REALLY CHARACTERIZED HIM THOUGH WAS THE FACT THAT HE UNDERSTOOD THAT BY MAKING HIS REVOLUTIONARY METHOD OF CUTTING HAIR AVAILABLE TO EVERY HAIRDRESSER IN THE WORLD BY OPENING SCHOOLS AND ACADEMIES HE COULD REALLY MAKE A LASTING DIFFERENCE IN THEIR LIVES. HE DID WITHOUT A DOUBT CHANGE THE WORLD AND WILL PROBABLY CONTINUE TO DO SO FOR MANY YEARS TO COME.

IN THE MID NINETIES, I BEGAN RESEARCHING A BOOK CALLED "HAIR HEROES." THE BOOK WAS AN HOMAGE TO THE GREATEST HAIRDRESSERS WHO EVER LIVED, SOME UNSUNG AND SOME REVERED; ALL OF WHOM HAD CHANGED THE FACE OF HAIRDRESSING FOREVER. FIVE YEARS LATER, WHEN I BEGAN TO WRITE THE BOOK, VIDAL AGREED TO BE ONE OF ITS TWELVE SUBJECTS. THIS WAS A TREMENDOUS HONOR, AND ALSO A NECESSITY, FOR NO ONE HAS REVOLUTIONIZED HAIRDRESSING LIKE VIDAL SASSOON.

I MET HIM AT HIS HOUSE IN BEVERLY HILLS WITH HIS WIFE RONNIE. OUR INTERVIEW COVERED ALL SORTS OF TOPICS, AND I WAS IMPRESSED BY HOW EDUCATED HE WAS, HOW THIRSTY FOR KNOWLEDGE, AND HOW GENEROUS WITH HIS TIME. AT ONE OF OUR BOOK SIGNING EVENTS IN SAN FRANCISCO, THE LINE WAS VERY LONG; CLOSE TO FIVE HUNDRED PEOPLE WHO'D LINED UP FOR FIVE HOURS. VIDAL WOULDN'T MOVE FROM THE TABLE TILL HE'D FINISHED EVERY SINGLE AUTOGRAPH. HE LOOKED EVERYONE IN THE EYE, SPOKE TO THEM, FOUND OUT SOMETHING ABOUT THEM, AND THEN VERY THOUGHTFULLY WROTE THE DEDICATION—SOME-THING WHICH I THINK PROBABLY CHANGED ALL OF THEIR LIVES. I WAS HOPEFULLY AS GENEROUS BUT A BIT MORE SPEEDY; I'D SIGN QUICKLY, WITH A "BIG LOVE FROM MICHAEL." NOT FOR VIDAL—HE REALLY WANTED TO GIVE THEM SOMETHING. HE WAS VERY AWARE OF HOW MUCH HIS TIME MEANT TO THEM; THAT ONE MINUTE WITH THEM COULD MAKE A TREMENDOUS DIFFERENCE TO THEIR LIVES FOREVER.

LATER ON, WHEN WE BECAME FRIENDS AND I DECIDED TO DO THIS BOOK AND A FILM TO CELEBRATE HIS EIGHTIETH YEAR, I BECAME MORE AND MORE CONSCIOUS OF HOW THIS GENEROSITY PERMEATED HIS ENTIRE LIFE, AND PROBABLY THE LIVES OF EVERY HAIRDRESSER IN THE WORLD. HE STANDS ALONE AS THE MOST

FAMOUS TO HAVE EVER LIVED. IT WASN'T JUST BECAUSE HE CREATED NEW SHAPES; HE CREATED A NEW TECHNIQUE WITH WHICH TO DO THE SHAPES. HIS SALONS WERE THE ANTITHESIS OF THE CHANDELIER PALACES WHERE I'D BEEN TRAINED; THEY WERE STEEL AND GLASS, WITH CLEAN, MODERN LINES. HE HAD A VISION, DEVELOPED IT, AND WORKED TIRELESSLY TOWARDS ITS FRUITION AND CONTINUED EVOLUTION. IT CANNOT BE OVEREMPHASIZED HOW SASSOON'S NEW STYLE LIBERATED WOMEN. NOT ONLY DID THEY LOOK DIFFERENT—NO LONGER SPORTING HELMETS OF HAIR—BUT THEY FELT EMPOWERED AND LIBERATED BY THE SURPLUS OF TIME, WHICH GAVE THEM A CHANCE TO CONSIDER CAREERS. VIDAL'S MODERN HAIRCUTS COULD LAST SIX TO EIGHT WEEKS, WHICH MADE THEM ACCESSIBLE TO ALL WOMEN IN ALL WALKS OF LIFE. SECRETARIES, TEACHERS, AND SHOP ASSISTANTS GOT THEIR HAIR DONE NEXT TO DUCHESSES AND COUNTESSES AT VIDAL SASSOON'S.

HE ESSENTIALLY DEMOCRATIZED HAIRDRESSING; NOT AN EASY THING TO DO IN LONDON WHICH HAS A VERY RIGID AND STIFF CLASS STRUCTURE. VIDAL WANTED TO SHARE EVERYTHING HE HAD. THE FAMILY TREE THAT SPREAD THROUGHOUT SASSOON TOUCHES ALMOST EVERY HAIRDRESSER IN THE WORLD IN SOME WAY. YOU CAN TRACE ALMOST ALL THE CURRENT HAIRDRESSERS BACK TO VIDAL OR SOMEONE WHO LEARNED THERE. PRIOR TO THIS, HAIRDRESSING USED TO BE SEQUESTERED, A PRIVATE AFFAIR; THE STAR STYLISTS LAUNCHED NEW LOOKS TO THE PRESS BUT NEVER DREAMED OF TEACHING IT. VIDAL'S VISION WAS TO COMPLETELY CHANGE THE WORLD AND EVERY HAIRDRESSER IN IT.

BY THE MID-EIGHTIES, VIDAL SASSOON HAD BECOME UBIQUITOUS. HE WAS A GLOBAL BRAND, RECOGNIZABLE ALL OVER THE WORLD. HE STOPPED CUTTING HAIR IN HIS MID-FIFTIES, AND ANNIE HUMPHRIES, CHRISTOPHER BROOKER, AND PHILIP ROGERS, TRUSTED MEMBERS OF HIS TEAM, TOOK OVER THE SALONS, SCHOOLS, AND ACADEMIES. HIS FAME GREW SO MUCH THAT HE MOVED TO THE USA, WHERE HIS STYLES HAD THE SAME IMPACT AS THEY'D HAD IN LONDON. HE WAS CONSTANTLY FEATURED IN FASHION MAGAZINES, FOR BOTH HIS WORK AND THE PHOTOGRAPHS OF HIM AT PARTIES, LOOKING INCREDIBLY CHIC. HE WAS REGULARLY FEATURED ON EVERY POPULAR TALK SHOW OF THE DAY, SUCH AS JOHNNY CARSON AND PHIL DONAHUE, AND HAD HIS OWN SHOW CALLED "YOUR NEW DAY." HE WAS WONDERFULLY ENGAGING AND ENERGETIC AS A HOST, BUT AFTER TWO YEARS, HE FELT THAT IT CONFINED HIM. HE WAS AND STILL IS SO PASSIONATE ABOUT POLITICS, SO CONCERNED ABOUT HELPING PEOPLE. BECAUSE OF HIS LACK OF A FORMAL EDUCATION, HE'S VERY CONCERNED THAT EVERYBODY GETS A GREAT EDUCATION, THAT PEOPLE HAVE THEIR BASIC NEEDS TO PROSPER AND GROW IN LIFE. HE SET UP THE CENTER FOR ANTI-SEMITISM IN ISRAEL AND BECAME AN AVID PHILANTHROPIST, WHILE STILL MANAGING TO TRAVEL THE WORLD, REPRESENTING PROCTOR AND GAMBLE, AND PROMOTING THE SASSOON BRAND IN ASIA WHERE IT IS STILL INCREDIBLY POPULAR.

WHEN HURRICANE KATRINA HIT, HE FOUND A NEW CAUSE. TO QUOTE HIM, HE WAS "OUTRAGED AT THE LACK OF OUTRAGE" ABOUT KATRINA—THE LACK OF CARE OR CONCERN THAT OUR GOVERNMENT SHOWED. HE DECIDED TO USE HIS HUGE CLOUT IN THE HAIRDRESSING INDUSTRY BY RAISING MONEY TO BUILD HOMES FOR PEOPLE WHO WERE HOMELESS. THIS IS SOMETHING HE CONTINUES TO DO TO THIS DAY. VIDAL IS, I WOULD SAY, A GREAT MAN. IT'S A GIFT AND HE KNOWS THAT WHEN YOU HAVE A GIFT, YOU SHOULD SHARE IT. I'M HOPING THAT THIS BOOK IS ABLE TO IMPART SOME OF THIS, AND, THAT BY SHARING IT WITH YOU, IT CAN INSPIRE YOU TO MAKE THE MOST OF YOUR LIVES.

CHILD
HOOD

AT THE AGE OF FIVE I WAS PUT IN AN ORPHANAGE; IF YOU HAVE A CHOICE, STAY AT HOME.

I WAS BORN IN SHEPHERD'S BUSH IN 1928, WHICH WAS A TIME WHEN NOT MANY PEOPLE DOWN OUR WAY HAD MONEY TO SPEND ON THEIR HEADS. MY FATHER LEFT WHEN I WAS FOUR AND MY BROTHER IVOR TWO, FORCING MY MOTHER TO WORK LONG HOURS IN A SWEATSHOP. DURING THE DAYS SHE WAS AT WORK, MY BROTHER AND I GOT INTO ALL SORTS OF TROUBLE; I REMEMBER BEING THOROUGHLY HAPPY MOST OF THE TIME. IT WAS, HOWEVER, NO WAY TO START LIFE; MY MOTHER KNEW WE NEEDED STRICT SUPERVISION WHICH SHE COULDN'T GIVE US UNLESS SHE LEFT HER JOB. SO WHEN I WAS FIVE, SHE RELUCTANTLY SENT ME TO AN ORPHANAGE IN MAIDA VALE. MY WILD DAYS OF PIRACY WERE OVER.

VIDAL   BETTY   IVOR

SHE TAUGHT ME ABOUT POSSIBILITIES WHICH CAN BECOME PROBABILITIES AND DID.

MY MOTHER DIED YESTERDAY. SHE HAD LIVED NINETY-SEVEN YEARS, THREE MONTHS, AND TWENTY-ONE DAYS. I'VE KNOWN HER ALMOST SEVENTY YEARS AND AT THIS MOMENT SHE IS GUIDING MY PEN, FOR HER INFLUENCE ON AND WITHIN ME WAS DEEP AND PROFOUND. MY FATHER WAS NOT AWARE OF US ALTHOUGH WE LONGED FOR HIS ATTENTION—A CHILD'S LOVE THWARTED; BOTTLED EMOTIONS WHICH ARE NEVER FULLY FREED, THE SOUL CARRIED THIS BURDEN AS WE DID FOR OUR FATHER. THERE WAS A NIGHT WHEN MOTHER WAS PENNILESS, FORCED TO EVACUATE HER HOME WITH IVOR AND ME. SHE COULD NOT FACE THE EMBARRASSMENT OF EVICTION, AND I WAS TOLD LATER WE LEFT AT TWO IN THE MORNING TO STAY WITH OUR AUNT KATIE WHO KINDLY TOOK US IN. MY MOTHER WAS A VICTIM OF THE TIMES AND ONE YEAR LATER MY BROTHER AND I LEFT AUNT KATIE FOR A JEWISH ORPHANAGE. IT WAS TO BE SIX YEARS LATER; I WAS ELEVEN. HITLER INVADED POLAND. BRITAIN WAS AT WAR WITH GERMANY. I HAVE STRAYED FAR IN TELLING YOU HOW I FELT ABOUT MY MOTHER BUT TO KNOW SOMETHING OF THE HARDSHIPS IS TO KNOW HER STRENGTHS. SHE HAS AND ALWAYS WILL HAVE IN MY THOUGHTS SUCH GREAT DIGNITY PERCHED HIGH ON A CHARISMATIC THRONE—HER PRESENCE, THE CONDITION OF HER BEING WERE EVIDENT TO ALL. I LOVED HER GRACE—SHE TALKED WITH ELOQUENCE BEYOND EDUCATION AND SHE TAUGHT FROM HER INNER KNOWLEDGE. SHE WAS A ZIONIST WHO GAVE ME PRIDE IN MY JEWISHNESS; SHE TAUGHT ME ABOUT "POSSIBILITIES" WHICH CAN BECOME PROBABILITIES AND DID. I OWE HER SO MUCH AND WHEN I SPEAK IN GLOWING TERMS OF A GREAT LADY IT IS BECAUSE SHE WAS AND IS. I KNOW NO ONE LIKE HER. MAMA THANK YOU. YOUR SON.

WINSTON CHURCHILL'S SPEECHES
HAVE NEVER BEEN ABLE TO BE EMU-
LATED. THERE WAS NAZI GERMANY
THAT CONTROLLED ALL OF EUROPE,
FRANCE HAD CAPITULATED AND THEN
THERE WAS BRITAIN, ALL ON ITS
OWN. THE ISOLATIONISTS IN AMERICA
DIDN'T WANT TO COME INTO THE WAR
THOUGH ROOSEVELT KNEW HE'D HAVE
TO EVENTUALLY. AND CHURCHILL,
WITH HIS GREAT MASTERY OF LAN-
GUAGE, SPOKE ON THE RADIO AND
I BELIEVE HE SAVED DEMOCRACY.
CHURCHILL WAS THE ONE SAYING IN
THE EARLY '30S, "WE HAVE TO DO
SOMETHING ABOUT ADOLF HITLER."
PACIFISTS CALLED HIM ALL SORTS OF
NAMES, AND WITH THE NUMBER OF
MEN KILLED IN WORLD WAR ONE, YOU
CAN UNDERSTAND IT. BUT HE HAD THE
VISION. EVENTUALLY BRITAIN MADE
HIM FIRST LORD OF THE ADMIRALTY,
THEN HE BECAME PRIME MINISTER
WHEN CHAMBERLAIN STEPPED DOWN.
WITHOUT QUESTION, HE SAVED
DEMOCRACY.

STATE

SMAN

I BELIEVE THAT CHURCHILL, WITH HIS MASTERY OF LANGUAGE, GOT TO THE ENGLISH PEOPLE AND SAVED DEMOCRACY.

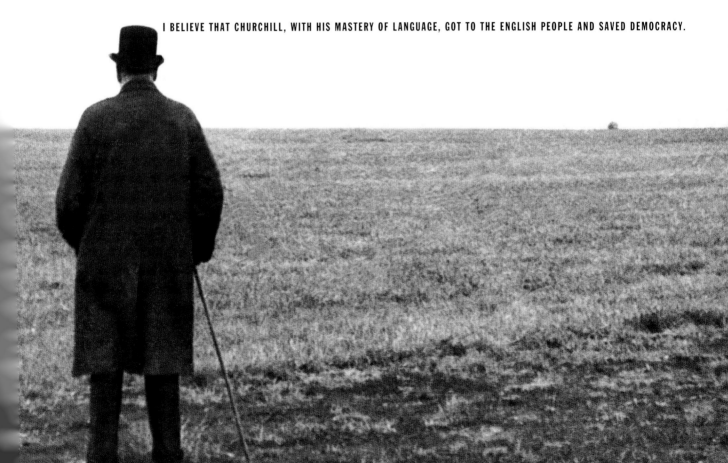

THE WAR WAS FRIGHTENING AND TERRIBLE
BUT IT WAS NORMAL LIFE FOR US; AFTER THE
ORPHANAGE WHAT WAS NORMAL LIFE ANYWAY?

ON SEPTEMBER 3RD 1939, BRITAIN AND FRANCE DECLARED WAR ON GERMANY BECAUSE OF POLAND. HITLER HAD MARCHED IN ON THE 1ST OF SEPTEMBER. SUDDENLY, ALL THE KIDS OF LONDON WERE PICKED UP AND SENT TO THE COUNTRY WHERE WE LIVED WITH COWS AND SHEEP FOR THE NEXT FEW YEARS. AND, OF COURSE, THE VERY NICE PEOPLE THAT TOOK US IN.

I CAME BACK TO LONDON AT 14, AND THE WAR WAS STILL ON; I WAS SLEEPING DOWN AT THE SHELTER, AS EVERYBODY DID. THE LUFTWAFFE WAS REARRANGING THE STREETS OF LONDON EVERY NIGHT, THE ARCHITECTURE IS CHANGING AT EVERY MOMENT; I GOT A JOB AS A BIKE MESSENGER, GOING FROM THE CITY ON A BIKE WITH NO UNIFORM, CARRYING A MESSAGE TO THE DOCKS.

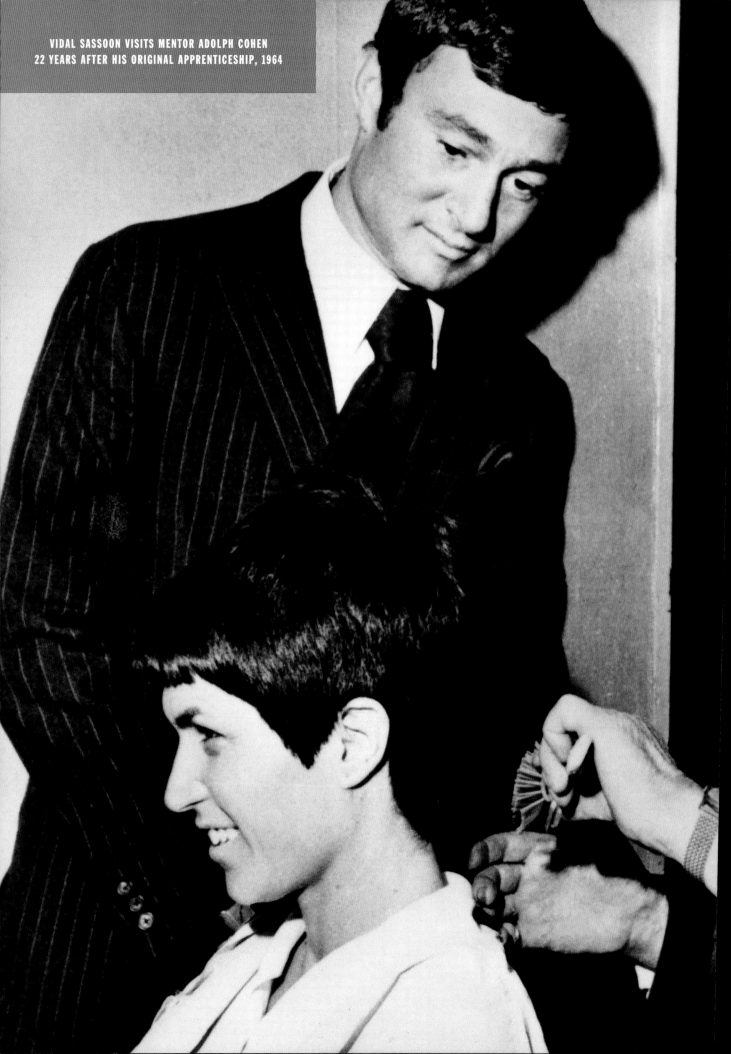

A MOTHER'S PREMONITION

WHEN I WAS 14, MY MOTHER TOOK ME TO A HAIRDRESSER NAMED ADOLPH COHEN. LATER ON, SHE TOLD ME THAT SHE'D DREAMT I'D BE A HAIRDRESSER. WHEN WE GOT TO HIS SALON, HE ASKED FOR A HUNDRED GUINEAS, WHICH WAS A HUNDRED POUNDS AND A HUNDRED SHILLINGS IN THOSE DAYS. MY MOTHER SAID, "WE DON'T HAVE A HUNDRED BUTTONS". I WAS RELIEVED BECAUSE I DIDN'T WANT TO BE A HAIRDRESSER. I OPENED THE DOOR ON THE WAY OUT AND DOFFED MY CAP TO MY MOTHER AND MR. COHEN. HE WAS SO IMPRESSED BY MY MANNERS THAT HE TOLD ME HE'D WAIVE THE FEE AND TO START MONDAY. I APPRENTICED FOR TWO YEARS WITH HIM. PRESSED TROUSERS EVERY MORNING, CLEAN NAILS, CLEAN SHOES— ALL IN THE MIDDLE OF A WAR. HE WAS A DISCIPLINARIAN AND HAD AN ENORMOUS EFFECT ON MY SENSE OF HOW WE SHOULD PROGRESS IN OUR CRAFT.

VIDAL EXHIBITING PRECISION STYLING IN A LOCAL HAIR COMPETITION, 1952

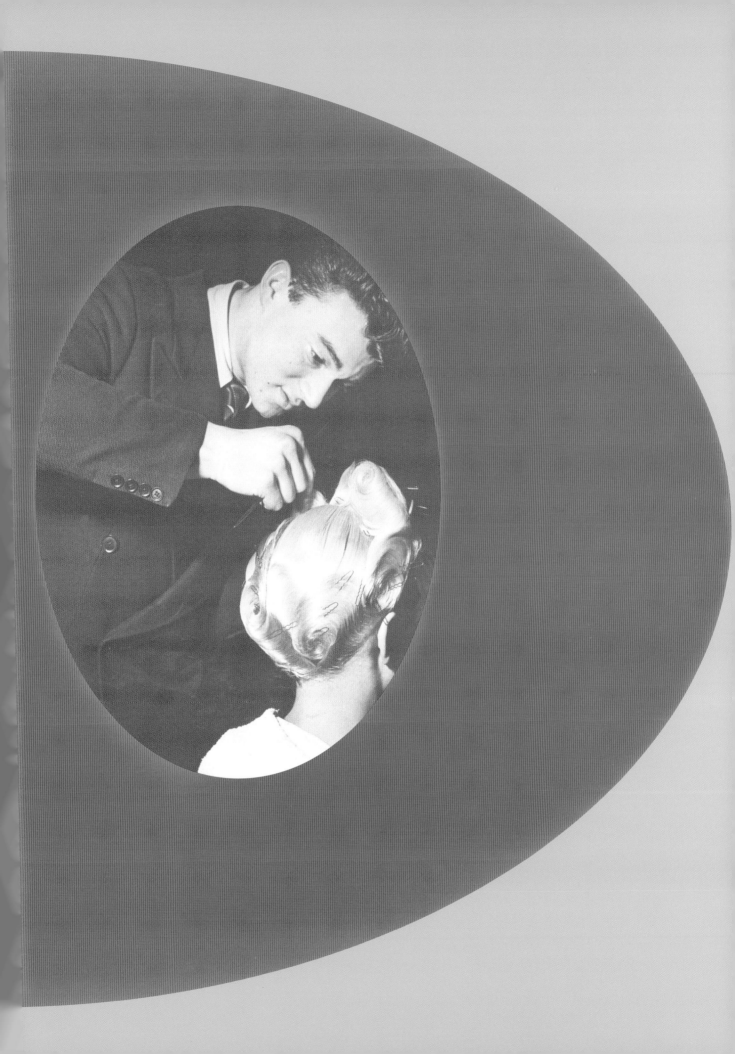

THE WAR WAS OVER. BRITAIN'S FASCISTS WERE RELEASED FROM INTERNMENT. SIR OSWALD MOSLEY WAS ON THE MARCH AGAIN, PREACHING HIS SICK OLD ANTI-SEMITIC SERMONS. QUITE A FEW FRIENDS OF MINE WERE DETERMINED TO STOP HIM, AND NATURALLY ENOUGH, I JOINED THEM IN THIS ENTERPRISE. THIS WAS THE 43 GROUP. WE WERE GIVEN ALL THE INFORMATION OF WHERE THE FASCISTS WOULD BE, WHERE THEY'D HAVE THEIR MEETINGS. WE WAYLAID THEM. WE DID SOME DAMAGE. AFTER THE HOLOCAUST, AFTER 6 MILLION JEWS WERE KILLED, YOU COULDN'T JUST SIT AT HOME AND ALLOW THESE THUGS TO BE RUNNING AROUND LONDON SCREAMING, "WE GOT TO GET RID OF THE YIDS."

JA

MO

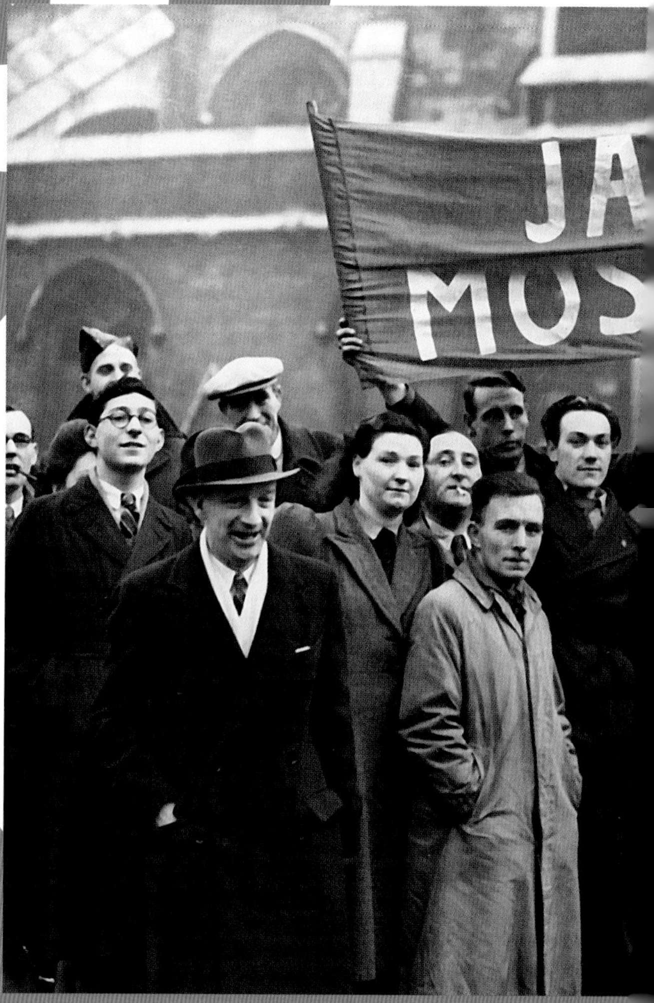

IN APRIL OF 1948, I ATTENDED A RECRUITMENT MEETING FOR THE ISRAELI WAR. THE SPEAKER TOLD US THAT IT WAS OUR JOB TO MAKE ABSOLUTELY CERTAIN THAT ISRAEL WAS A STRONG COHESIVE NATION THAT COULD AGAIN HOUSE ITS DIS-PLACED PERSONS AFTER THE WAR—THAT THEY WOULD NEVER KNOW PERSECUTION, OCCUPATION, OR DEGRADATION. AT THE TIME, ARAB FORCES WERE TRYING TO INVADE ISRAEL AND RAID THE COMMUNITIES. UNDER THE UNITED NATIONS MANDATE, THE NEGEV DESERT BELONGED TO ISRAEL. HOWEVER, HALF OF IT WAS UNDER ARAB CONTROL, AND SEVERAL THOUSAND EGYPTIAN TROOPS WERE FIRMLY EMBEDDED THERE, HAVING REFUSED TO WITHDRAW WHEN THE STATE OF ISRAEL WAS PROCLAIMED. I DECIDED TO GO. THE EGYPTIANS ATTACKED CONSTANTLY, BUT WE FOUGHT DAY AND NIGHT, WITH NO FOOD OR WATER, AND EVENTUALLY OUR POSITION IN THE GAZA STRIP WAS IMPREGNABLE. THERE WAS TALK OF THE UNITED NATIONS MOVING IN AND A CEASE-FIRE. WHEN I GOT BACK TO LONDON, I REALIZED THAT THOSE MONTHS IN THE DESERT HAD HELPED ME TO GROW UP AND HAD GIVEN ME A NEW, MORE SENSIBLE SET OF VALUES.

FOR THE FIRST TIME IN MY ADULT LIFE, I FELT AS THOUGH I BELONGED. I WAS FREE FROM ANTI-SEMITISM AND DISCRIMINATION.

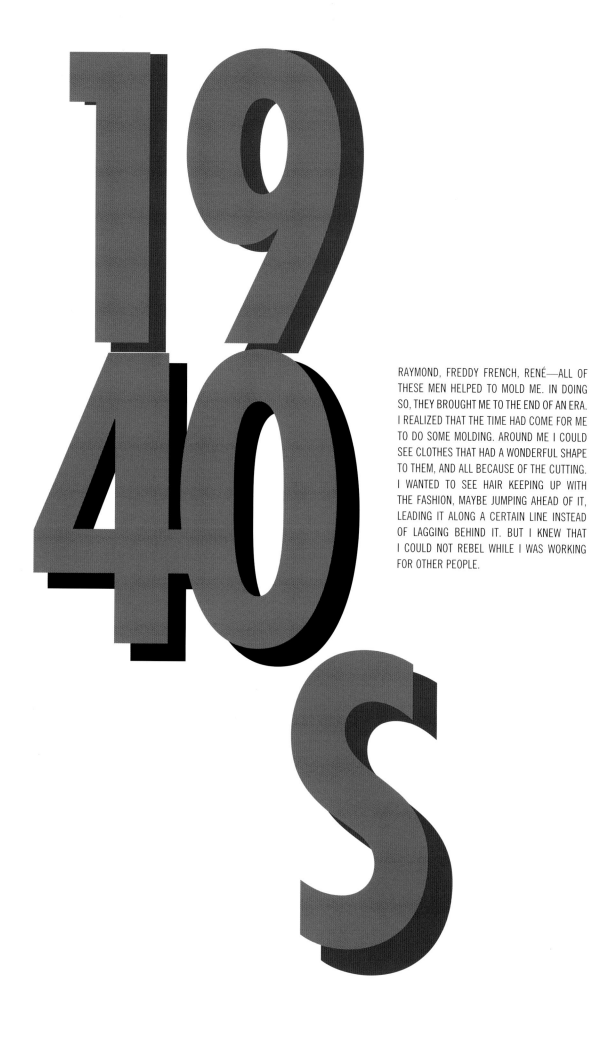

1940s

RAYMOND, FREDDY FRENCH, RENÉ—ALL OF THESE MEN HELPED TO MOLD ME. IN DOING SO, THEY BROUGHT ME TO THE END OF AN ERA. I REALIZED THAT THE TIME HAD COME FOR ME TO DO SOME MOLDING. AROUND ME I COULD SEE CLOTHES THAT HAD A WONDERFUL SHAPE TO THEM, AND ALL BECAUSE OF THE CUTTING. I WANTED TO SEE HAIR KEEPING UP WITH THE FASHION, MAYBE JUMPING AHEAD OF IT, LEADING IT ALONG A CERTAIN LINE INSTEAD OF LAGGING BEHIND IT. BUT I KNEW THAT I COULD NOT REBEL WHILE I WAS WORKING FOR OTHER PEOPLE.

HIS SENSE OF FRUSTRATION AT BEING CONFINED BY
THE TIME WAS MOST EVIDENT. HE WAS SO DRIVEN
IN HIS SEARCH. **HAROLD LEIGHTON**

EVEN IN THE EARLY FIFTIES, WHEN VIDAL AND I WORKED IN EDGWARE ROAD AT SALON ROMAINE, YOU COULD SEE HIS ENORMOUS DRIVE. THE SEEDS OF WHAT HE WAS LOOKING FOR WERE VISIBLE. HE SEEMED HAUNTED BY IT. ON OCCASION HE WOULD GET SO FRUSTRATED THAT HE'D THROW THE BRUSH OR COMB AWAY. NEVER A PAIR OF SCISSORS BECAUSE THEY WERE THREE POUNDS, SIX DOLLARS IN THOSE DAYS. THAT WAS EXPENSIVE. HE WOULD JUST LEAVE THE CLIENT, WALK OUT OF THE SALON, AND GO FOR A WALK. AND SOMETIMES HE WOULDN'T COME BACK INTO THE SALON, SOMETIMES HE WOULD.
HAROLD LEIGHTON

I LEARNED CUTTING TECHNIQUE FROM RAYMOND, OR "TEASY-WEASY," A GREAT CUTTER WHO PRUNED, SHAPED, ANGLED, CUT, DID IT ALL WITHOUT USING SHEARS, OR RAZORS.

IT WAS SOMETHING THAT WAS ARTISTIC, NEW TO THE CRAFT. HE HAD A METHOD OF CUTTING THAT WAS BEAUTIFUL—I RESPECTED HIM ENORMOUSLY FOR IT.

MONSIEUR RENÉ WAS A TALL, CHIC FRENCH-MAN WHO HAD PLAYED PROFESSIONAL FOOTBALL FOR FRANCE AS A GOALKEEPER. HIS SALON CATERED TO THE COGNOSCENTI—THE FAMOUS PEOPLE IN FASHION, ARTS, POLITICS, AND FINANCE IN LONDON. HE OOZED FRENCH CHARM AND LOVED TO HAVE A LINEUP OF INCREDIBLE-LOOKING WOMEN READY TO GET HIS ATTENTION.

RENÉ OF MAYFAIR AND ZSA ZSA GABOR, 1960

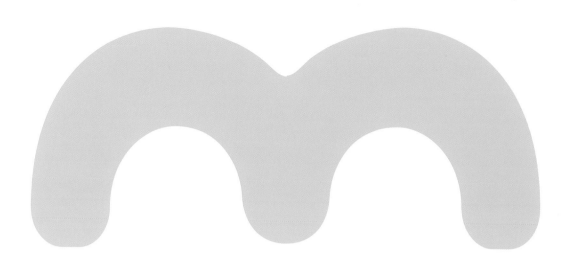

FOTOSEARCH

FOTOSEARCH

BOUFFANT

1950s HAIRDRESSING MEANT WEEKLY OR BIWEEKLY TRIPS TO THE SALON, WHERE HAIR WAS BLOWN, SPRAYED, SHELLACKED, SET AND SPRAYED EVEN MORE; THEN MAINTAINED WITH GREAT CARE AND ATTENTION, WHICH MEANT A LIMITED LIFESTYLE. VIDAL'S CUTS ALLOWED FOR A WHOLE NEW WAY OF LIFE; THEY GAVE WOMEN MORE TIME AND MORE FREEDOM TO PURSUE ANY LIFESTYLE THEY CHOSE. NO LONGER TETHERED TO THEIR SALON VISITS, THEY WERE ABLE TO GET WASH-AND-WEAR CUTS ONCE A MONTH. IT WAS AN INTEGRAL PART OF WOMEN'S LIBERATION.

108 BOND STREET

I WANTED TO BE IN ON THE REVOLUTION THAT WAS SIMMERING, BUT I KNEW THAT I COULD NOT REBEL WHILE WORKING FOR OTHER PEOPLE. SO, I LEFT RAYMOND AND DID NOT LOOK FOR ANOTHER JOB. INSTEAD I LOOKED FOR A SALON OF MY OWN.

IT WAS A SMALL PLACE, WITH FEW CLIENTS AT FIRST. BUT AFTER A WHILE, UPHOLDING THE STANDARDS OF SERVICE I LEARNED FROM ADOLPH COHEN AND THE TECHNIQUES OF CUTTING I LEARNED FROM RAYMOND, I BUILT A CLIENTELE. IT GOT BUSY, VERY BUSY. WE QUICKLY OUTGREW OUR TINY SALON.

BUT DESPITE THE SUCCESS, I KNEW THERE WAS SOMETHING MORE. IT WAS THE FIFTIES. HAIR WAS STILL DRESSED AND TEASED. IT DIDN'T LOOK MODERN. CLOTHES STARTED TO LOOK MODERN, THE THEATER CHANGED, PEOPLE'S ATTITUDES CHANGED. IT BECAME, VERY MUCH, A POST-WAR SOCIETY FILLED WITH NEW IDEAS. HOW COULD I DO THE SAME IN HAIR? THEN, I BECAME EXPOSED TO SOMETHING NEW. SOMETHING CLEAN AND PURE, A STUDY OF ANGLES, SHAPES AND FORM. I SAW THE NEW BAUHAUS AND INTERNATIONAL SCHOOL OF ARCHITECTURE APPEAR ALL OVER THE GLOBE.

NINE

I MARRIED A DIVINE LADY. ELAINE WAS MY RECEP-
TIONIST. SHE WAS A WELSH GIRL, AND SHE WAS
TALL, BLONDE, ELEGANT, DELIGHTFUL. AND SHE
COULD STAND ONLY ABOUT EIGHTEEN MONTHS OF
ME, AND THEN SHE GAVE UP. I WAS NEVER THERE.
AND I WASN'T MARRIED AGAIN UNTIL I WAS 39 OR
40 BECAUSE I NEEDED THOSE TEN YEARS TO
DEVELOP THE CREATIVITY, THE CRAFT THAT WE
WERE TRYING TO CHANGE. I NEEDED THAT TIME.

THERE WERE
MOMENTS WHEN I
FELT I WAS ON
THE VERGE OF A
BREAKTHROUGH.
THEN SOMETHING
WOULD GO WRONG
AND I WOULD FEEL
SICK WITH. . .

THAT WAS MY INSPIRATION—THE BAUHAUS, ARCHITECTURE. I'M NOT FILM-STRUCK BUT I'M ARCHITECTURE-STRUCK WHEN I SEE GREAT ARCHITECTS AND WHAT THEY DO AND HOW THEY CHANGE CITIES. IF I HAD TO HAVE HEROES AT ALL, IT WOULD BE GREAT ARCHITECTS. APART FROM THE FACT THAT IT WOULD HAVE BEEN WONDERFUL TO HAVE BEEN A GREAT ARCHITECT, THE CRAFT HAS BEEN SO GOOD TO ME AND I'VE LOVED IT. WORKING ON A SUBSTANCE THAT YOU CAN MOLD AND SHAPE IS TOTALLY FASCINATING. HAIR IS THE ONLY SUBSTANCE THAT YOU CAN DO THAT WITH. IT GROWS FROM THE HUMAN FORM IN SO MANY DIFFERENT WAYS ON DIFFERENT HEADS.

PHOTO BY VIC SINGH

FOR ME, THE
WORKING OF HAIR
IS ARCHITECTURE
WITH A HUMAN
ELEMENT

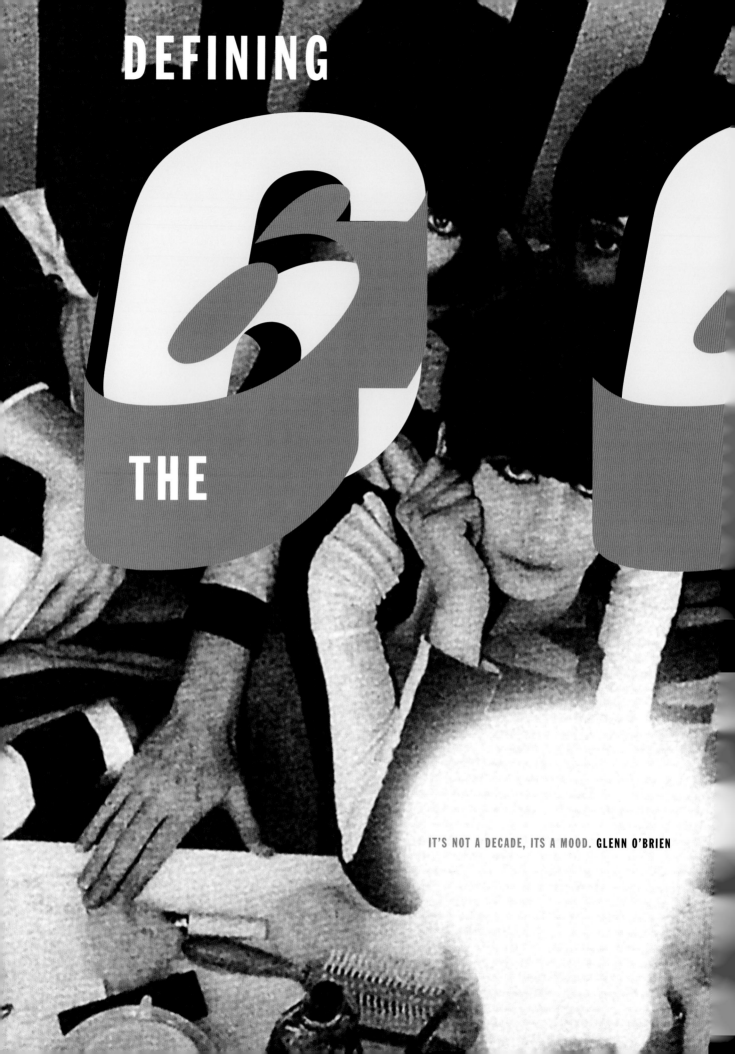

DEFINING

THE

IT'S NOT A DECADE, ITS A MOOD. GLENN O'BRIEN

PHOTO BY HENRI DAUMAN

NO MORE WAR. HAD ENOUGH OF THAT. NO MORE PINSTRIPE, BOWLER HAT, UMBRELLA 9 TO 5. IT'S A NEW WORLD, A NEW FRONTIER, A NEW THING. IT'S ELECTRIC AND AMPLIFIED. ELECTRIC CIRCUS, ELECTRIC FLAG, ELECTRIC ZOO, ELECTRIC ELECTRIC. STATIC. FEEDBACK. HAIR DOWN TO THERE, SKIRT UP TO HERE. BAND OF GYPSIES EMERGING FROM THE GRAY MASSES, DAY-GLO AND VELVET, PAINTED FACES TRAVELING FROM ANCIENT DAYS TO FUTURE PERFECT. IT'S A TRIP—A TRIP THAT'S SO FAR OUT IT'S IN. GLENN O'BRIEN

THE SIXTIES WAS ALL IN THE HEAD. HEADS. SO MAYBE IT IS STILL GOING ON SOMEWHERE. MAYBE ON A PLANET ORBITING THAT STAR UP THERE NEXT TO...WOW, IS IT A FULL MOON? **GLENN O'BRIEN**

IN 1957, MARY QUANT CAME IN AND I GAVE HER A HAIRCUT. FIRST TIME I'VE EVER NIPPED SOMEBODY'S EAR, AND IT WAS HERS. I SAID, "I'LL TELL YOU WHAT, THIS MAKES US BLOOD BROTHER AND SISTER..."

WE HAD SOME GREAT COLLABORATIONS IN LONDON WITH FASHION'S MOST EXCITING NEW DESIGNERS, SUCH AS MARY QUANT. WHAT A THRILLING TIME. IT REALLY SEEMED LIKE THE CENTER OF IT ALL!

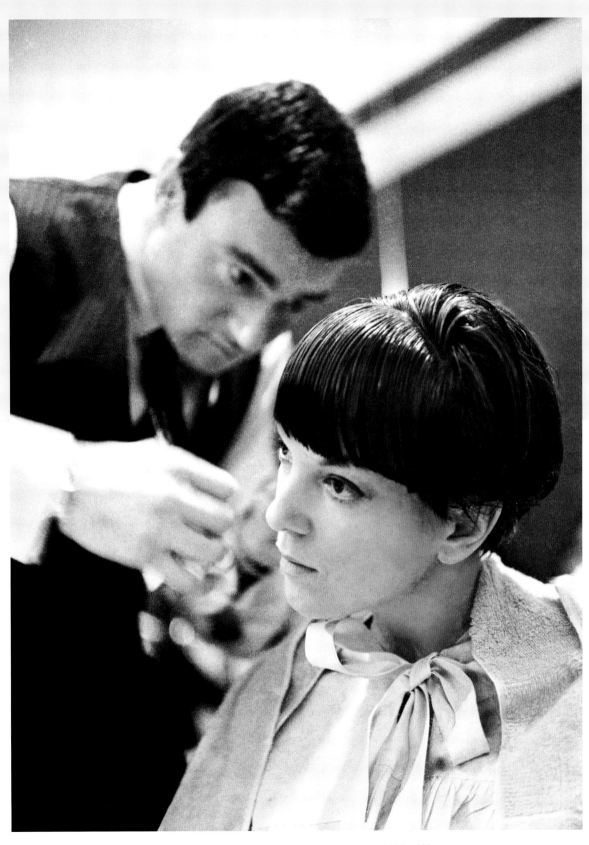

VIDAL WITH CLIENT AND COLLABORATOR MARY QUANT, 1963

MARY

THE FIRST TIME I SAW A VIDAL SASSOON HAIRCUT, I WAS RIVETED. I LOOKED IN THE WINDOW, WENT UPSTAIRS, AND SAW VIDAL FLAMBOYANTLY DOING SOMEONE'S HAIR, WAVING HIS SCISSORS, DANCING AROUND THE CHAIR. I MADE UP MY MIND THEN AND THERE THAT I WAS GOING TO SAVE UP THE MONEY TO COME BACK TO HIM AND HAVE MY HAIR CUT. I BECAME A CLIENT. EVERYBODY HAD COME TO LONDON TO BE CREATIVE WHETHER THEY WERE ACTORS, PHOTOGRAPHERS, WRITERS…ALL OF THE ARTS. LONDON BECAME THAT MARVELOUS MELTING POT OF IDEAS. IT WAS AN EXTRAORDINARY TIME. AND SO UNIQUE—COMING OUT OF THE DRABNESS OF THE WAR, THE DOOM AND GLOOM; LIFE WENT FORWARD AND WE WERE ABLE TO DO AS WE WANTED BECAUSE NOBODY WAS DOING ANYTHING. SO WE MADE WHAT WE WANTED AND WHAT WE NEEDED. THE POWER, THE MERITOCRACY WAS YOUTH. THEY CALLED IT THE "YOUTH QUAKE." **MARY QUANT**

PHOTO BY DAVID BAILEY

QUANT

MARY WORKING IN HER KINGS ROAD STUDIO

YOU HAVE NO IDEA WHAT KING'S ROAD
WAS LIKE IN THE 60s. IT WAS LIKE THE
WHOLE STREET WAS HER ATELIER.

I WANTED TO CUT HAIR AS THEY CUT CLOTH. I
WANTED TO SHAPE HEADS AS THE NEW YOUNG
FASHION DESIGNERS WERE SHAPING BODIES.

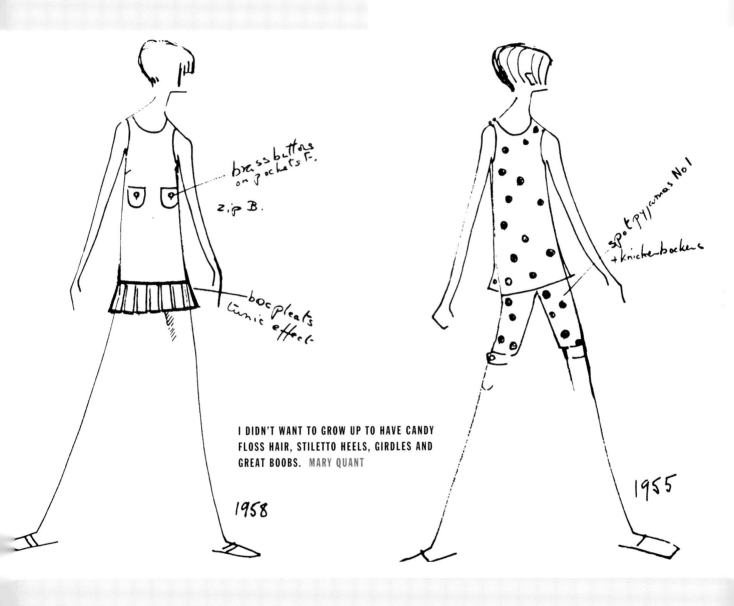

brass buttons
on pockets F.

zip B.

boc pleats
tunic effect.

spot pyjamas No1
+ knicker-bockers

I DIDN'T WANT TO GROW UP TO HAVE CANDY
FLOSS HAIR, STILETTO HEELS, GIRDLES AND
GREAT BOOBS. MARY QUANT

1958

1955

NANCY

I GOT A CALL FROM A FILM PRODUCTION COMPANY TO ASK: WOULD I CUT NANCY KWAN'S HAIR. SHE JUST MADE A GREAT FILM WITH WILLIAM HOLDEN WHICH WAS A BIG SUCCESS. SHE CAME IN, GORGEOUS GIRL, WITH FOUR FEET OF HAIR DOWN HER BACK. I STARTED TO CARVE INTO THIS BEAUTIFUL HAIR AND I SAW THAT BY BRINGING THE BACK UP SLIGHTLY AND KEEPING THE LENGTH AT THE SIDES, YOU'D GET A GREAT ANGLE FROM THE SIDE, AND SHE COULD SHAKE IT AND IT WOULD FALL INTO PLACE. SHE WAS PETRIFIED. SHE PLAYED CHESS WITH HER MANAGER WHILE ALL THIS WAS HAPPENING—SHE COULDN'T LOOK. BUT I WAS SEEING SOMETHING. IT WAS THE ARCHITECTURAL SENSE OF WHAT WE WERE DOING—MAKING A STATEMENT, AS I USED A BARBER'S SHEARS ON THAT MAGNIFICENT ROPE OF BLACK HAIR, SHE NEVER EVEN RAISED HER HEAD. SHE MOVED ONLY WHEN SHE STRETCHED OUT A HAND TO MOVE ONE OF HER CHESSMEN. SHE WON AND I THINK THAT I WON, TOO.

PHOTO BY HENRI DAUMAN

AS THE SALON GREW, IT BECAME SO MUCH BUSIER AND THE WHOLE OF LONDON WAS BEGINNING TO
EXPLODE. KING'S ROAD, THANKS TO MARY QUANT AND ALEXANDER PLUNKET-GREENE, WAS INCREDIBLE.
ENGLAND WAS SUDDENLY BECOMING AN EXTREMELY IMPORTANT PART OF FASHION, BEAUTY, HAIR,
THE THEATER, AND EVERYTHING ELSE, WHICH WAS EXCITING BECAUSE IT TOOK A LONG TIME TO
RECOVER FROM THE SECOND WORLD WAR. LAURANCE TAYLOR

PEGGY COULD ACT OUT THE CLOTHES SO EXTRAORDINARILY. THE SHAPE SHE MADE WITH HER BODY! SHE WAS JUST PHENOMENAL.

PHOTO BY WILLIAM CLAXTON

"I FIRST MET VIDAL WHEN HE WAS IN NEW YORK TO OVERSEE THE OPENING OF THE NEW SALON. THERE WAS THIS LITTLE PICTURE OF A HAIRCUT IN THE NEWSPAPER CALLED THE WASH AND WEAR. I WAS ENCHANTED WITH THE IDEA OF WASH AND WEAR. AND I THOUGHT, "THAT'S THE WAY I WANT MY HAIR TO BE." PEGGY MOFFITT

INTERNATIONAL MODELS
PEGGY MOFFITT
AND
TWIGGY
TOGETHER IN 1968.
PEGGY'S HAIR BY VIDAL.
TWIGGY'S HAIR BY LEONARD LEWIS.

IT WAS A TIME WHEN ALL THE NEW MODELS WANTED TO GET IN ON THE NEW LOOK. IT WAS EASY TO GET HOUSE MODELS BECAUSE GIRLS WANTED TO LOOK HIP, AND HAIRCUTS WERE WHAT HAPPENED. I WAS FORTUNATE TO WORK WITH SUCH MODELS AS GRACE CODDINGTON.

VIDAL SASSOON WITH GRACE CODDINGTON, ONE OF HIS EARLIEST HOUSE MODELS ON WHOM HE DID SOME OF HIS BREAKTHROUGH CUTS. SHE BECAME ONE OF THE MOST IMPORTANT FASHION EDITORS IN THE WORLD.

PHOTO BY DAVID BAILEY

71

DAVI
D
BAI-
LEY

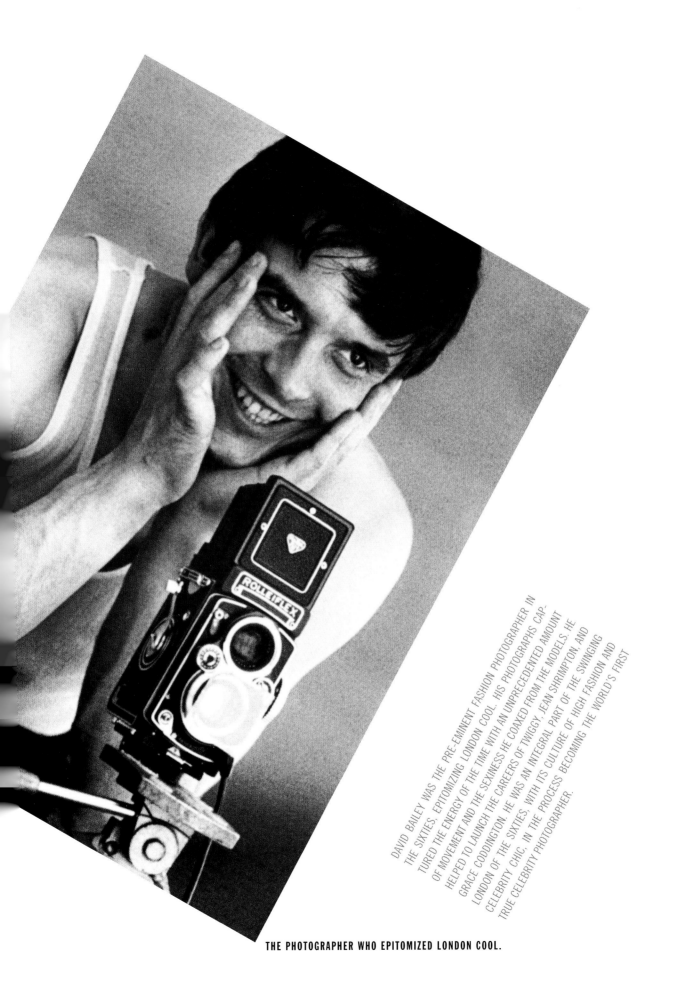

DAVID BAILEY WAS THE PRE-EMINENT FASHION PHOTOGRAPHER IN THE SIXTIES, EPITOMIZING LONDON COOL. HIS PHOTOGRAPHS CAPTURED THE ENERGY OF THE TIME WITH AN UNPRECEDENTED AMOUNT OF MOVEMENT AND THE SEXINESS HE COAXED FROM THE MODELS. HE HELPED TO LAUNCH THE CAREERS OF TWIGGY, JEAN SHRIMPTON, AND GRACE CODDINGTON. HE WAS AN INTEGRAL PART OF THE SWINGING LONDON OF THE SIXTIES, WITH ITS CULTURE OF HIGH FASHION AND CELEBRITY CHIC, IN THE PROCESS BECOMING THE WORLD'S FIRST TRUE CELEBRITY PHOTOGRAPHER.

THE PHOTOGRAPHER WHO EPITOMIZED LONDON COOL.

BOND STREET DESIGNED BY DAVID HICKS

I WANTED TO CHANGE THE WHOLE THING. I DIDN'T WANT TO BE A HAIRDRESSER TO BEGIN WITH. IF MY MOTHER HADN'T BROUGHT ME TO ADOLPH COHEN WHO KNOWS WHAT I WOULD HAVE BECOME? THE WHOLE LOOK OF SALONS BOTHERED ME—THE PINK WALLS, THE CHANDELIERS, THE POSH CLIENTS, THE TEASED HAIR—IT JUST WASN'T WHAT THE WORLD WAS ABOUT ANY MORE. SO WE CHANGED THE WAY THEY LOOKED. BOND STREET DIDN'T LOOK LIKE A SALON; IT LOOKED LIKE A MODERN ART GALLERY. WE CHANGED THE WAY WE CUT HAIR; WE FOCUSED ON SHAPES AND ANGLES THAT WOULD BRING OUT THE BONE STRUCTURE AND DID AWAY WITH THE ADORNMENT AND TEASING. IT BECAME ABOUT THE CUT, NOT JUST THE STYLING. WE HAD A YOUNG, COOL, GOOD-LOOKING TEAM THAT DRESSED OUT OF THE PAGES OF MAGAZINES. WE LOWERED PRICES SO ALMOST ANYONE, NOT JUST UPPER-CLASS LADIES, COULD AFFORD TO GET THE NEW LOOK RIGHT ON BOND STREET—ON THE POSH END OF BOND STREET! WE DID ALL OF THIS WHILE MAINTAINING HIGH STANDARDS OF WORK AND SERVICE; WE DIDN'T OPEN A FAST FOOD OPERATION. WE INVENTED A NEW WAY OF WORKING WHILE KEEPING THE OLD STANDARDS OF SERVICE AND QUALITY. EVEN WHEN WE EXPANDED, WE DID THIS BY CREATING A METHOD AND TEACHING IT.

BOND STREET

EMMANUELLE KHAN, ONE OF THE MOST EXCITING DESIGNERS IN FRANCE, FLEW OVER SPECIALLY FROM PARIS SO THAT I COULD CUT HER HAIR; AFTER THAT THERE WERE QUITE A FEW PEOPLE CALLING IT THE KHAN CUT.

Charles of the Ritz

VIDAL SASSOON

COMING TO NEW YORK AND BEING ABLE TO OPEN SALONS THERE WAS BEYOND WHAT I HAD EVER IMAGINED, BUT IT OPENED ALL SORTS OF POSSIBILITIES FOR MORE PEOPLE TO BE PART OF THE EXPANSION, AND THE ENERGY WAS EXPLOSIVE. OUR GRAND OPENING AT CHARLES OF THE RITZ IN NEW YORK CITY WAS SLATED TO BE OCTOBER OF 1964. WE MORE REALISTICALLY PREDICTED CHRISTMAS. IN ACTUALITY, IT WAS SPRING OF 1965. OUR MAIN WORRY WAS TRAINING; SOME OF OUR STAFF HAD ONLY BEEN IN THE BUSINESS FOR THREE OR FOUR YEARS. BUT WE SUCCEEDED, THANKS TO OUR PUPILS. IF WE WORKED HARD, THEY WORKED HARDER. THEY NEVER LOST THEIR ENTHUSIASM. AND BY THE TIME WE HAD FIN- ISHED WITH THEM, WE KNEW WE HAD A TEAM OF HAIRDRESSERS WE COULD PIT AGAINST THE WORLD, DESPITE THE FACT THAT THEIR AVERAGE AGE WAS ONLY TWENTY-TWO.

IN ANY INDUSTRY, CRAFT OR ART, YOU NEED TO SPEND MORE TIME AT IT IF YOU WANT TO BECOME BETTER THAN THE AVERAGE. IT'S NOT A 9:00 TILL 5:00 THING. IT COULD BE A 14-HOUR DAY BY THE TIME YOU'RE FINISHED WITH YOUR MODELS, AND THEN YOU GO TO WORK THE FOLLOWING DAY. SO, MY SENSE WAS THAT I HAD TO BE MINDFUL. I WASN'T A VEGETARIAN, BUT I WAS VERY CAREFUL WITH FOOD. I EXERCISED, ALWAYS HAVE. WHEN I WAS OVERTIRED, AS ONE WOULD BECOME, I'D GO TO PLACES LIKE GRAYSHOTT HALL AND DO THE FULL 10-DAY TREATMENT. THAT WAS MARVELOUS BECAUSE YOU'D GO THERE, AND FOR THREE OR FOUR DAYS, THEY'D STARVE YOU, LITERALLY—WATER AND A CUP OF TEA AT 4 O'CLOCK. WELL, IT WAS IN ENGLAND.

PHOTO BY HENRI DAUMAN

YOUR GUIDE TO BEAUTY & HEALTH

BY BEVERLY & VIDAL SASSOON

DAILY EXPRESS

A YEAR OF HEALTH
AND BEAUTY

VIDAL AT HOME IN LOS ANGELES TAKING A DAILY SWIM 2008

CONTRARY TO PUBLIC OPINION, HAIRDRESSING IS NOT A SOFT LIFE. THOUGH SOME PEOPLE THINK OF HAIRDRESSERS AS FRAGILE, PAMPERED PEOPLE, I BELIEVE THAT ANY MAN WHO DOES FIFTEEN HEADS A DAY—ON HIS FEET ALL THE TIME, REMEMBER—DESERVES HEAVY WORKERS' RATIONS WHETHER THE SALON IS ON BOND STREET, IN BATTERSEA, OR THE BACK STREETS OF BROOKLYN. THAT IS WHY I'VE ALWAYS GONE OUT OF MY WAY TO KEEP MYSELF FIT. SOME MAY CALL ME FUSSY, BUT SINCE I BEGAN THIS ROUTINE, I HAVE FELT FAR FITTER, FOR LIKE MY HAIRCUTS, IT WORKS.

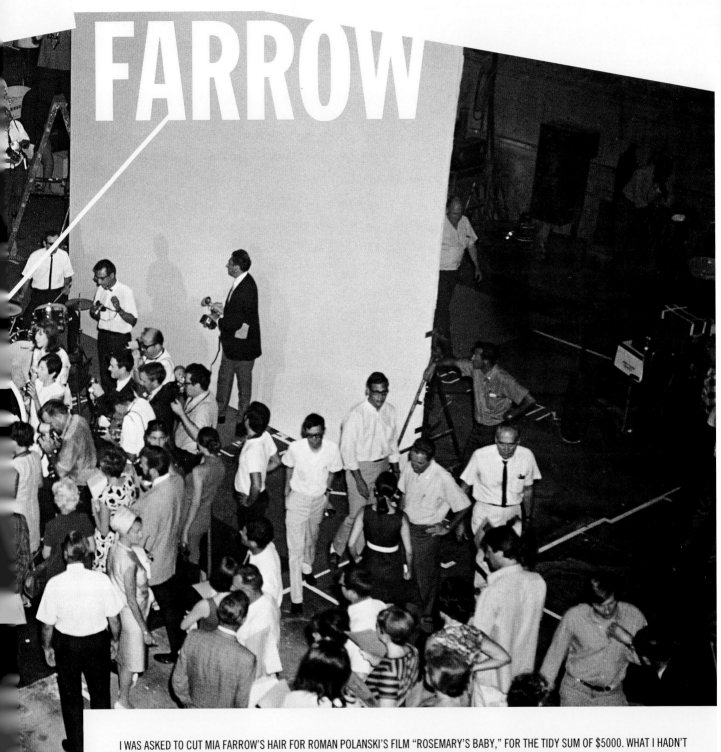

FARROW

I WAS ASKED TO CUT MIA FARROW'S HAIR FOR ROMAN POLANSKI'S FILM "ROSEMARY'S BABY," FOR THE TIDY SUM OF $5000. WHAT I HADN'T ANTICIPATED, HOWEVER, WAS THAT OVER A HUNDRED JOURNALISTS HAD BEEN INVITED TO RECORD THE EVENT, TO BE PHOTOGRAPHED IN A STUDIO SPACE. AT ONE-THIRTY PRECISELY I LED MIA ONTO STAGE THIRTEEN. SOMEWHERE A JAZZ QUARTET WAS PLAYING COOL, COOL MUSIC. SOMEWHERE MUCH NEARER, THE MOVIE CAMERAS BEGAN TO WHIR. I PUT A TOWEL AROUND MIA. I PICKED UP MY SCISSORS. I MADE THE FIRST CUT, FEELING LIKE A HIGH PRIEST AT A ROYAL SACRIFICE. THE FIRST LOCK OF FARROW HAIR HAD SCARCELY HIT THE APRON WHEN THE PRESS WERE DOWN FROM THEIR SEATS, ACROSS THE TWENTY YARDS TO THE ROPES, OVER THEM AND ON TOP OF US. THEY WEREN'T JUST BREATHING DOWN MY NECK, THEY WERE DAMN NEAR BREAKING IT. AND ALL THE TIME I WAS DANCING AROUND THAT SMALL, BLONDE HEAD, SNIPPING HERE, FLICKING A COMB THERE, USING THE RING, JOSTLING AND BEING JOSTLED, WHILE THE FLASH BULBS POPPED AND THE JAZZ BAND PLAYED, UNHEARD NOW AND FORGOTTEN. IT WAS A PSYCHEDELIC SCENE.

TO ME, HAIRDRESSING MEANS SHAPE. THEREFORE IT'S VERY IMPORTANT THAT THE FOUNDATIONS BE RIGHT. AS SOON AS I SAW MIA, I KNEW I WAS GOING TO HAVE NO TROUBLE. HER BONE STRUCTURE IS SUPERB—HER CHEEKBONES, HER JAWLINE. HER EARS, TOO, ARE SMALL AND NEAT, AND FOR A HAIRCUT WITH NO HOLDS BARRED, THAT IS A GREAT HELP.

THE SALON AT 171 BOND STREET WAS A BREAKTHROUGH IN THE DESIGN OF HAIR SALONS; NO LONGER ORNATE, CHANDE-LIERED PALACES, DAVID HICKS' DESIGN FOR THE SALON WAS A SERIES OF SLEEK SHAPES AND MATERIALS—CHROME, GLASS, DARK WOOD. HE USED WHITE ON THE FLOOR, WALLS AND CEILINGS, BLACK ON MURALS, DRESS-ING TABLES, MIRROR FRAMES, SHAMPOO BASIN AND DROP LIGHTSHADES. HE GAVE A FEELING OF SPACE TO THE ENTRANCE FLOOR BY PUTTING IN AN OPEN-TREAD STAIRCASE WITH BLACK BANISTERS LEADING UP TO A MEZZANINE FLOOR TO FORM A BALCONY. VIDAL CHOSE HICKS FOR HIS USE OF COLOR, AND WILLINGNESS TO TAKE RISKS, WHICH HAD BROUGHT A FRESH LOOK TO THE STALE DESIGN ENVIRONMENT. HICKS WAS KNOWN TO JUXTAPOSE A MODERN ABSTRACT PAINT-ING WITH CLASSICAL URNS OR VASES, OR TO PLACE ANTIQUE SCULPTURES ON PLEXI-GLASS BASES. PERIOD FRENCH FAUTEUILS WOULD BE UPHOLSTERED IN BOLD MODERN PATTERNS. EXPENSIVE OBJETS D'ART WOULD SIT IN A TABLESCAPE NEXT TO ORDINARY FOUND OBJECTS FROM A BEACH OR A RUIN. IT WAS PRECISELY THE KIND OF WORK AND THINKING TO COMPLEMENT VIDAL'S RADICAL IDEAS AND THEIR FRUITION IN THE SALON.

THE

WITH AN EXTRAORDINARY ARTISTIC TEAM WE WERE ABLE TO CREATE A HAIRCUTTING ART FORM.

DREAMTEAM

IN THE SIXTIES MY COLLEAGUES AND I INHALED THE VIGOR OF LONDON WHERE HIGH ENERGY WAS THE NORM, IDEAS WERE ECLECTIC AND ELASTIC AND WE STRETCHED THEM TO THE LIMIT. INSPIRATION OWES MUCH TO A GUT REACTION TO ANY GIVEN SITUATION AND I AM CONSTANTLY ELATED BY THE EFFICACY OF HAIR AS AN ART FORM AND BY THE CONTINUOUS PART WE HAVE PLAYED IN BRINGING THIS ABOUT.

THE EVOLVING EXCITEMENT OF THE PAST 40 YEARS, THE FIDELITY OF AN IDEAL AND SHEER ARTISTRY OF TIM HARTLEY, ANNIE HUMPHREYS, ROGER THOMPSON, CHRISTOPHER BROOKER AND MANY OTHERS HAS GIVEN OUR LONDON BEGINNINGS A WORLDWIDE REPUTATION. BUT MOST OF ALL I AM PROUD OF THE FACT THAT WE HAVE TRAINED THOUSANDS OF PEOPLE FROM ALL NATIONS, DEVELOPING TALENTS AND MINDS, WHICH HAVE HELPED BEAUTIFY THIS WORLD AND HAVE GIVEN OUR CRAFT INTERNATIONAL CREDIBILITY AND DIGNITY.

THE TEAM AT 171 BOND STREET, 1969

ONE OF VIDAL'S BIGGEST TALENTS WAS INSTILLING IN PEOPLE A PURPOSE, EITHER WITHIN HIM OR WITHIN THEIR OWN RIGHT. HE NEVER PUSHED PEOPLE TO THE POINT THAT THEY BECAME MECHANICS; THOUGH A LOT OF PEOPLE THINK IT'S A MECHANICAL THEORY, IT REALLY ISN'T. HE ALWAYS LEFT THE SPACE FOR SOMEBODY TO GO THROUGH AND THAT'S THE BIG DIFFERENCE. THEY'VE ALL CREATED THEIR OWN IMAGE. THEIR OWN LIVES FROM THAT, AND THEY'RE RESPECTED FOR IT. MAURICE TIDY

ROGER

ROGER WAS MY RIGHT HAND. AND THE FIRST INTERNATION-
AL ART DIRECTOR OF VIDAL SASSOON. HE WAS SO TALENTED
HE COULD ACTUALLY CUT WITH BOTH HANDS. WHEN WE
OPENED THE SALON AT THE GROSVENOR HOUSE I INSISTED
THAT HIS NAME WAS ON THE DOOR ALONGSIDE MINE.

WATCHING ROGER WAS WATCHING A
GENIUS AT WORK. **TREVOR SORBIE**

ROGER'S SOFTNESS, HIS WHOLE BODY LANGUAGE, THE WAY
HE CUT HAIR, YOU COULD JUST STAND AND WATCH HIM.
AND UNDERNEATH ROGER WAS CHRISTOPHER BROOKER
WHO IN TIME PROCEEDED TO BE IN THE POSITION OF
NUMBER ONE, THE CREATIVE ART DIRECTOR. VIDAL WAS
CLEVER BECAUSE HE LEFT A VERY, VERY SOLID TEAM
OF CREATIVE PEOPLE, WHO ARE THERE TO THIS DAY.
TREVOR SORBIE

CHRISTOPHER BROOKER WAS AN INTELLECT—A WORLD-CLASS CHESS PLAYER, SO THAT GIVES YOU AN IDEA WHAT HIS BRAIN IS LIKE. CHRISTOPHER WASN'T AS COMMUNICATIVE AS ROGER OR VIDAL, AND IT WAS HARD TO KNOW HIM. BUT HIS IDEAS WERE BRILLIANT, AND I THINK HE WAS RESPONSIBLE FOR THE MAJOR HAIRCUTS THAT CAME OUT OF SASSOON IN THE SEVENTIES. **TREVOR SORBIE**

CHRISTOPHER WAS THE SECOND INTERNATIONAL ART DIRECTOR OF VIDAL SASSOON, AND WHILE VERY
DIFFERENT FROM ROGER HIS IMPACT ON THE COMPANY WAS ALSO HUGE. HE WAS RESPONSIBLE FOR
SOME OF THE INCREDIBLE NEW DIRECTIONS IN HAIR.

VIDAL SASSOON WAS THE BEST TEACHER AND THE GREATEST WHO HAS EVER LIVED. HE HAS BEEN THE BEST
AMBASSADOR OF OUR INDUSTRY. CHRISTOPHER BROOKER

CHRISTOPHER BROOKER

BREAKT

IT WAS THE GEOMETRY AND THE ANGLES AND THAT SENSE OF NEWNESS—WORKING TO BONE STRUCTURE RATHER THAN MAKING PEOPLE LOOK PRETTY. WITH A GREAT HAIRCUT THEY COULD SHAKE IT, BRUSH IT, DO WHATEVER THEY WANTED AND IT WOULD FALL INTO PLACE. THIS CHANGED THE CRAFT. CUT TO BONE STRUCTURE IS THE ARCHITECTURE OF HAIR.

IT TOOK NINE YEARS, FROM 1954 TO 1963, TO BREAK THE MOLD OF THE HAIRDRESSING THAT WAS.

I REGARD THE FIVE POINT CUT AS THE FINEST CUT I HAVE EVER CREATED, THE GEOMETRIC DESIGN IN ITS PUREST, MOST CLASSICAL FORM.

A VISUAL ART FORM DEVELOPED THROUGH MIRRORS WHICH OPEN WINDOWS FOR MANY.
I SEE PEOPLE AS SHAPES, BONE STRUCTURES, AS ANIMATED SUBJECTS FOR THE SCISSORS.
IF THERE WAS A PERSONAL INFLUENCE, IT WAS BAUHAUS, BUT IT ALL HAD TO BE DONE WITH A
PAIR OF HANDS. BEING A VISUAL ART, HAIR IS FAR MORE EMOTIONAL. ITS MISTAKES BROUGHT
TEARS, STILL DO, ITS ACHIEVEMENTS, LAUGHTER AND HAPPINESS. HOW LUCKY TO BE ABLE TO
TOUCH A HUMAN BEING, TO BE EXHILARATED BY A CRAFT THAT IS CONSTANTLY CHANGING,
TO HAVE THAT SUBSTANCE WHICH GROWS FROM THE HUMAN FORM THAT YOU CAN MOLD TO
CREATE SPONTANEOUS FASHION, AND YET BRING OUT THE INDIVIDUALITY. HOW LUCKY I HAVE
BEEN TO BE INVOLVED IN THE POETRY OF CHANGE.

PHOTO BY BARRY LATEGAN

IN 1974, VIDAL WAS ASKED TO DO A SHOW IN PARIS—THE FIRST TIME THAT AN ANGLO-SAXON HAIRDRESSER HAD BEEN ASKED. THE FRENCH DON'T BRING OUTSIDERS IN BECAUSE THEY THINK THAT THEY'RE BEST, AND IN A WAY, THEY ARE. VIDAL PULLED ALL HIS ART DIRECTORS TOGETHER AND SAID, "LOOK GUYS, THIS IS A BIG SHOW FOR ME. WE'RE GOING TO PARIS. WE NEED A COLLECTION OF HAIRCUTS." WE ALL WENT OUR SEPARATE WAYS AND GOT BUSY EXPERIMENTING ON NEW LOOKS; ONE DAY, I TRIED TO DO A HAIRCUT, WHICH WAS ONE LENGTH TO THE TOP OF THE EAR AND THEN VERY, VERY SHORT IN THE NAPE, BUT ALL ONE LENGTH. I LOOKED AT IT AND I SAID, "OH, GOD, THE FRENCH WOULDN'T LIKE THAT," BECAUSE THEY LIKE SOFT HAIR, FOR WOMEN TO LOOK LIKE WOMEN IN THE OLD-FASHIONED WAY. I DID THIS HAIRCUT—IT LOOKED A LITTLE BIT LIKE A HELMET. I THOUGHT, "NO, THAT'S NOT GOING TO WORK." I TRIED TO SALVAGE IT AND I JUST BRUSHED IT BACK BY CHANCE AND OUT CAME THIS PYRAMID SHAPE. AND THAT WAS THE BIRTH OF THE WEDGE HAIRCUT. IT WAS THE FIRST HAIRCUT TO EVER GET A DOUBLE-PAGE SPREAD IN ENGLISH VOGUE. THE REASON IT WORKED WAS IT COULD BE WORN BY MEN AND WOMEN—A CROSS-OVER TYPE OF HAIRCUT. AT THE SHOW, WHEN MY HAIRCUT CAME OUT, THE WEDGE, SHE WALKED DOWN THE CATWALK AND THE FRENCH HAIRDRESSERS LITERALLY PULLED HER OFF THE STAGE TO CHECK THE HAIRCUT, TO SEE HOW IT WAS CUT. THAT WAS REALLY WHAT GOT ME ON THE MAP IN HAIRDRESSING. TREVOR SORBIE

THE WEDGE

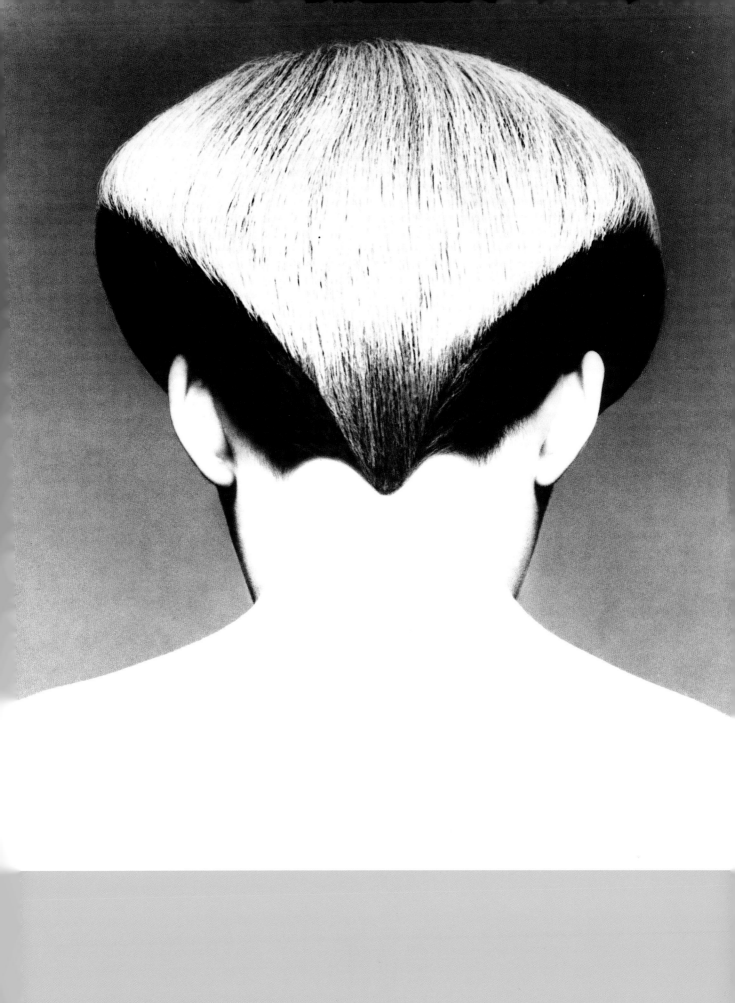

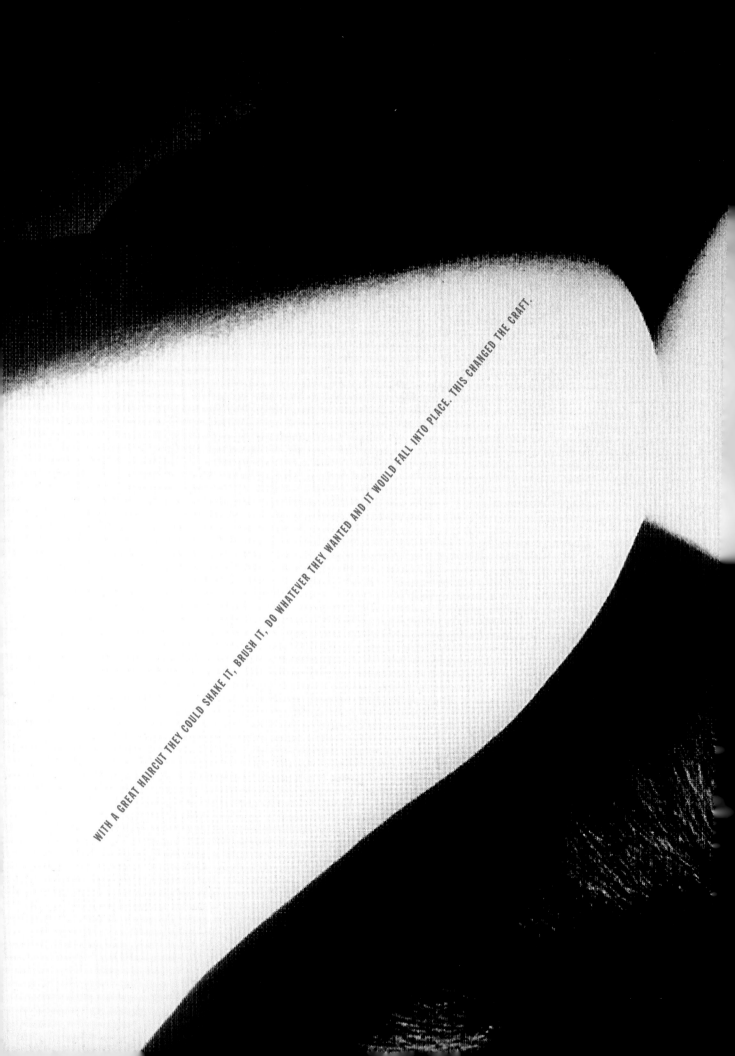

WITH A GREAT HAIRCUT THEY COULD SHAKE IT, BRUSH IT, DO WHATEVER THEY WANTED AND IT WOULD FALL INTO PLACE. THIS CHANGED THE CRAFT.

THE BRUSH

BY CHRISTOPHER BROOKER, 1973

THE QUIFF BY CHRISTOPHER BROOKER, 1972
PHOTO BY KARL STOECKER

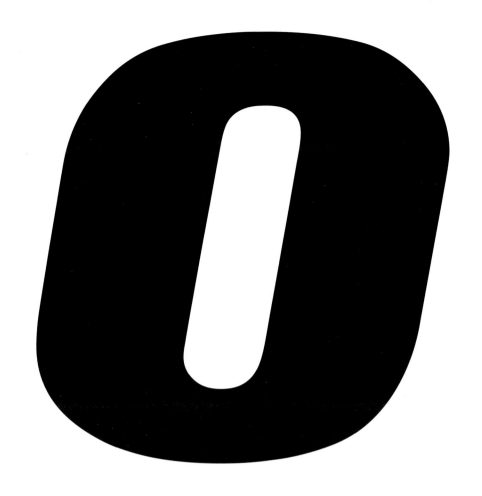

VIDAL TAUGHT ME SIMPLICITY AND WHAT THAT MEANS, AND THAT IT'S THE COMMON LINK TO ALL OBJECTS OF BEAUTY. TIM HARTLEY

BOX BOB BY FUMIO

MY INSPIRATION FOR JOINING SASSOON WAS THE SIMPLE, CLEAN LINE OF THE GEOMETRIC CUT. AFTER A FEW SOFTER STYLES BECAME POPULAR, I WANTED TO GO BACK TO SOMETHING MORE DEFINED WITH STRAIGHT LINES. MANY NEW DESIGNERS WERE SHOWING FASHIONS WITH CLEAN SIMPLE LINES AND I THOUGHT THE BOX BOB WOULD COMPLEMENT THIS. VIDAL SASSOON IS MY MENTOR AND INSPIRATION. WHAT HE DID FOR HAIRDRESSING CAN NEVER BE EQUALED AND I AM LUCKY TO HAVE BEEN ABLE TO BE THERE TO LEARN AND SHARE THIS TURNING POINT IN HISTORY. THE BOX BOB WAS TO HONOR THE MEMORY OF SASSOON'S BREAK-THROUGH CUTTING TECHNIQUE. SASSOON IS MY HERO AND MENTOR; ALWAYS HAS BEEN AND ALWAYS WILL BE. FUMIO KAWASHIMA

PHOTO BY JOHN SWANNELL

THE
BOX
BOB

TIMELESS

THE
BOX BOB
FIFTH AVENUE NYC
2008

5

FIVE

GRACE CODDINGTON

POINT

STYLE

MR. SASSOON IS EXTRAORDINARILY CHIC AND REEKS WITH STYLE. RICHARD BUCKLEY

PEOPLE COMING IN FROM SO MANY DIFFERENT COUNTRIES, SO MANY DIFFERENT CULTURES, LEARNING THE METHODS, TAKING THEM BACK TO THEIR OWN COUNTRIES TO UTILIZE THEM. IT ACTUALLY BROUGHT OUT A LOT OF ARTISTRY IN PEOPLE. ISN'T THAT MUCH MORE OF A DEED TO LIVE ONE'S LIFE THAT WAY RATHER THAN KEEPING AND DYING WITH THOSE SECRETS? NO, IF IT WAS SOMETHING WORTHWHILE, MAKE IT INTERNATIONAL. IF YOU'VE GOT SOMETHING WORTHWHILE THAT YOU CAN SPREAD INTERNATIONALLY, MY GOD, YOU DON'T KEEP IT. THEN IT DIES WITH YOU. YOU TEACH. YOU OPEN ACADEMIES, AS WE DID IN 1967.

SASSOON ACADEMY

I REMEMBER HE WOULD APPEAR ON T.V. AND BE INCREDIBLY CHARMING; HE USED TO DO THAT WONDERFUL THING WHERE HE CUT A WOMAN'S HAIR, SHE'D SHAKE HER HEAD AND IT WOULD FALL BACK INTO EXACTLY THE SAME PLACE, AND HE'D SAY "THIS IS WHAT CUTTING IS ALL ABOUT." I THOUGHT IT WAS ABSOLUTELY FANTASTIC.
PROFESSOR CAROLINE COX

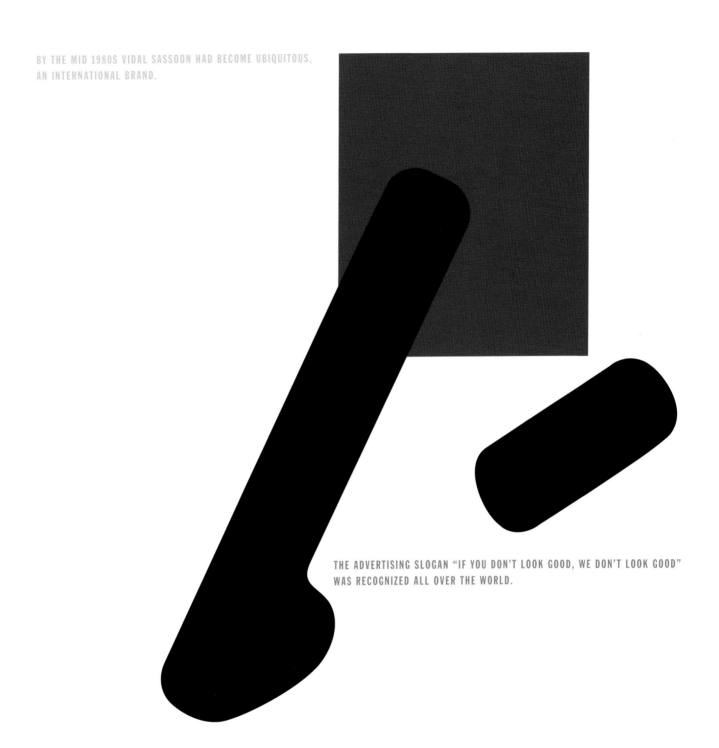

BY THE MID 1980S VIDAL SASSOON HAD BECOME UBIQUITOUS,
AN INTERNATIONAL BRAND.

THE ADVERTISING SLOGAN "IF YOU DON'T LOOK GOOD, WE DON'T LOOK GOOD"
WAS RECOGNIZED ALL OVER THE WORLD.

VIDAL APPEARED ON EVERY TALK SHOW ON T.V. AND HOSTED HIS OWN SHOW "YOUR NEW DAY"
HE WAS A HOUSEHOLD NAME.

$400 000 000
IN SALES
3000 EMPLO
50 COUNTRI
30 SALONS
8 SCHOOLS

I BOUGHT THE PRODUCTS BECAUSE I WANTED TO BE A PART OF THAT INTELLIGENT GLAMOUR.
PROFESSOR CAROLINE COX

YEES
ES

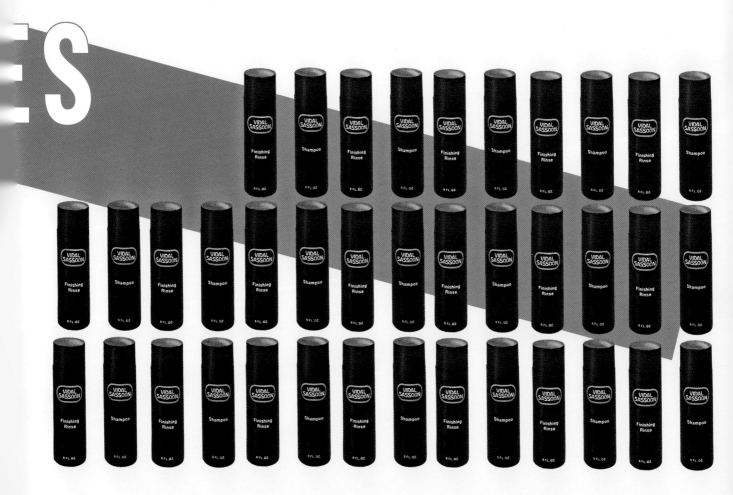

Their cuts are all-important

Sassoon

Bewitchingly bewigged

Guillaume

WAUKESHA FREEMAN

'The' Style Is Called Sassoon

The Way to Beauty

Hairstylist Looks to Future

DENVER POST

Hair Styling Has Been Road to Fame

Oh, Mr. Sassoon, bob me quick!

THE TELEGRAM

THE PHILANTHROPIC HAIRDRESSER

Sassoon peddles ideas as well as shampoo

Sassoon finds beauty in sharing

Sassooning: it's the latest thing in philanthropy

Vidal Sassoon crusades to end anti-Jewish bigotry

Los Angeles Times

Young Hairdressers Rule England's Hair Waves

BY PAT HAMMOND

Hairdressers Rule Britain's Hair Waves

Vidal Sasson tries to combat bigotry through education

The Philadelphia Inquirer

A Virtuoso Performance

VIDAL SASSOON INTRODUCES MASS MARKET SKIN CARE IN 3 SIMPLE STEPS

'All I Want for Graduation Is a Sassoon Cut!'

VIDAL and onetime wife Beverly at party Sybil Christopher gave to celebrate publication of his book, "Sorry I Kept You Waiting, Madam."

SUNDAY NEWS

NEW YORK'S PICTURE NEWSPAPER

THE PRESS DEMOCRAT

Dealers Feature Sassoon

Geometrics Add Up to Success

Hair Stylist Makes Mark With Geometric Effects

etti...g physical!

The Philadelphia Inquirer

Vidal Sassoon
puts a bold face on philanthropy

Utica Observer-Dispatch

American Hair-dos 'A Joke'?

America's Hairdos 'Bad Joke.' Says Britain's Sassoon

Jewish Books

The Atlanta Journal

SPOTLIGHT ON VIDAL SASSOON

A young Englishman makes good. In fact, he makes history! This is his success story, from its beginning right up to the present – with a peek at the future!

Youngstown Vindicator
Peninsula News
Learning to look terrific at any age

campaign

The Sassoon beauty empire launches its latest offensive

Vidal Sassoon Turns His Touch to Philanthropy

Utica Observer-Dispatch

America's Hairdos 'Bad Joke.' Says Britain's Sassoon

Stylist And State Get Into Hair Pulling Match

Hair-dos 'A Joke'?

The 'WRAPPED LOOK'

In for Spring: Short Hair

and Sleeker

SUNDAY NEWS
NEW YORK'S PICTURE NEWSPAPER

His Hairstyles Set New Pace

A Real Fashion 'Youthquake'

The Utmost In Madness

CALIFORNIA PILOT

Sassoon moves west

Hair Stylist Borrows From Arts To Re-Design Woman's Image

What A Difference A Few Changes Make

Olympic Swimming Stars Get 'Sassooned'

The Detroit News
Happiness is a cut at Vidal Sassoon's

SASSOON JADED, WITH THE GEOMETRIC CURLS

Dayton News
Sassoon Doesn't Mind Being Copied: It's Good Business

DIAGONAL CUT SLANTS ACROSS BROW
Latest Paula Considine Cut, Unseen

Venture Clubs To Convene

Philadelphia A La Sassoon

Sassoon In New York

PHOTO BY BARRY LATEGAN

I HAVE AN INTERESTING, WONDERFUL FAMILY—THEY THINK, THEY'RE INTUITIVE, THEY DO GREAT THINGS. MY DAUGHTER, EDEN, JUST OPENED A PILATES STUDIO HERE IN THE CITY. SHE'S DELIGHTFUL. MY OLDEST BOY, ELAN, IS DOING SOME EXTRAORDINARY THINGS IN OUR CRAFT. HE'S OPENING UP SALONS AND SCHOOLS WITH SOME LOVELY PEOPLE IN BOSTON, AND THEY'RE MOVING AROUND THE STATES. AND HE'S ABSOLUTELY LOVING IT. HAD THINGS TURNED OUT DIFFERENTLY, HE WOULD HAVE BEEN RUNNING THE COMPANY RIGHT NOW, BUT THAT'S NOT THE WAY IT WAS MEANT TO BE. I HAVE ANOTHER SON, DAVID, WHO WE ADOPTED WHEN HE WAS 3. HE WENT TO COLLEGE, DID BEAUTIFULLY—A DELIGHTFUL, INQUISITIVE YOUNG MAN. JUST THREE WEEKS AGO, I WAS 80. I TOOK THE WHOLE FAMILY DOWN TO CABO. IT WAS A BEAUTIFUL WEEK.

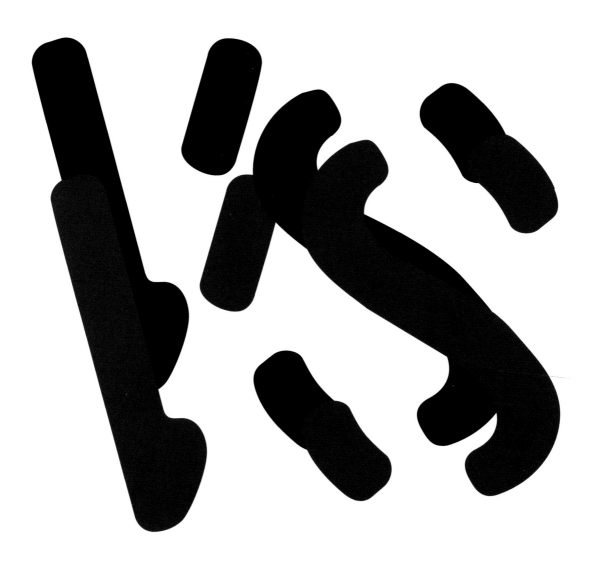

VIDAL SPENDS MOST OF HIS TIME IN HIS HOUSE
IN LA, WHERE HE STILL SWIMS A MILE A DAY.
HE TRIES TO GO TO LONDON AT LEAST TWICE
A YEAR. HE ATTENDS THE THEATER AS OFTEN
AS POSSIBLE DUE TO HIS GREAT LOVE FOR THE
DRAMATIC ARTS. IN 2011, HIS BIOGRAPHICAL
DOCUMENTARY WAS RELEASED AND HE WROTE
HIS MEMOIRS WHICH WERE PUBLISHED BY
MACMILLAN. HE IS STILL BUSY, ACTIVE, AND
THE UNDISPUTED HERO OF HAIRDRESSING.

CHELSEA IS THE FOOTBALL TEAM I'VE SUPPORTED SINCE I WAS A KID. NOT ONLY IS THE GAME BEAUTIFUL, BUT IT'S BETTER THAN THE PSYCHIATRIST'S COUCH BECAUSE YOU COULD SCREAM, YOU COULD SHOUT, YOU CAN SAY WHATEVER YOU WANT TO—GET ALL OF YOUR EMOTIONS OUT. IT'S A GAME THAT KEEPS PEOPLE SANE BECAUSE IT TAKES YOU OUT OF YOURSELF. YOU'RE IN A WHOLE OTHER WORLD, AND IT TAKES YOU OUT OF YOUR MIND AND INTO SOMETHING DIFFERENT. IT'S SIMILAR TO A GAME OF CHESS, AND PURE BALLET. SO, FOOTBALL IS VERY IMPORTANT IN MY LIFE.

VIDAL ON THE PITCH AT STAMFORD BRIDGE,
HOME OF CHELSEA FOOTBALL CLUB 2007

HE WAS VERY INVOLVED IN MY SOCCER PLAYING BECAUSE HE'S A HUGE SOCCER FAN, A CHELSEA FANATIC. WHEN MY BROTHER AND I WERE KIDS, HE WAS CONSTANTLY AT OUR GAMES. HE WAS VERY ENTHUSIASTIC AND WE WERE GOOD, SO WE PLAYED AND HE COACHED FOR MANY YEARS. HE TRAVELED FREQUENTLY FOR BUSINESS WHEN WE WERE GROWING UP, BUT HE'D ALWAYS COME BACK FOR A SOCCER GAME. IT WAS GREAT. ELAN SASSOON

PHI

THR

LANY

OPY

AN EXTRAORDINARY LADY NAMED MARY RECTOR GOT 6000 HAIRDRESSERS TO JOIN FORCES WITH HABITAT FOR HUMANITY—BUILDING HOUSES FOR THOSE WHO WERE LEFT WITH NOTHING. SHE GALVANIZED THE AMERICAN HAIRDRESSING COMMUNITY TO BE GENEROUS AND THEY REACTED WITH OPEN HEARTS AND POCKETS. TO THIS DATE, 23 FAMILIES ARE LIVING IN NEWLY BUILT HOUSES OF THEIR OWN.

RONNIE AND VIDAL

IT'S NICE TO BE WITH SOMEONE YOU ADMIRE AND WHO FASCINATES YOU.

I MET RONNIE WHEN I WAS 62, AND SHE WAS A DELIGHTFUL 30-SOMETHING. I WAS INVITED TO A DINNER PARTY IN CINCINNATI BY ONE OF THE VPS OF PROCTOR AND GAMBLE. SUDDENLY, THIS GIRL WALKS IN. NOT ONLY WAS SHE BEAUTIFUL, BUT HAD A PERSONALITY THAT YOU COULDN'T STOP BUT SIT AND LISTEN TO WHAT SHE HAD TO SAY. THERE WAS SOMETHING ABOUT HER THAT WAS EVEN HARD TO DESCRIBE. LET'S SAY FASCINATION AND I'VE BEEN FASCINATED EVER SINCE. WE'VE BEEN TOGETHER FOR 17 YEARS. WE WERE MARRIED 15 YEARS AGO, AND WHEN SHE'S NOT WITH ME, I ALWAYS SENSE HER AROMA. SHE'S ALWAYS THERE.

MY GORGEOUS WIFE. HER AWARENESS AND SUPERB EYE HAVE UPGRADED MY LEVEL OF CONSCIOUSNESS, ESPECIALLY IN THE ARTS. RONNIE HAS CAPTURED MY HEART AND OVERRULED MY HEAD. I MET HER IN 1989 AND HAVE NEVER LOOKED BACK.

HAIR
HERO

I AM A VERY LUCKY HAIRDRESSER

ON JUNE 13, 2009, QUEEN ELIZABETH II RECOGNIZED VIDAL SASSOON WITH AN AWARD—A CBE FOR HIS SERVICES TO THE BRITISH HAIRDRESSING INDUSTRY. THE CBE, WHICH STANDS FOR THE COMMANDER OF THE ORDER OF THE BRITISH EMPIRE, RECOGNIZES DISTINGUISHED SERVICE TO THE ARTS AND SCIENCES, PUBLIC SERVICES OUTSIDE THE CIVIL SERVICE AND WORK WITH CHARITABLE AND WELFARE ORGANIZATIONS OF ALL KINDS. VIDAL IS ONE OF THE FEW INDIVIDUALS WHO QUALIFIES FOR ALL THREE: HIS CONTRIBUTION TO THE WORLD OF FASHION AND THE ARTS, HIS INVOLVEMENT IN COMMUNITIES BOTH WORLDWIDE AND CIVIC, AND HIS MANY PHILANTHROPIC EFFORTS, RANGING FROM HURRICANE KATRINA RELIEF TO THE INTERNATIONAL CENTER FOR RESEARCH OF ANTI-SEMITISM, WHICH HE FOUNDED IN JERUSALEM, AND THE VIDAL SASSOON ACADEMIES, WHICH HAVE TRAINED HUNDREDS OF THOUSANDS OF HAIRDRESSERS AROUND THE WORLD.

STEVE HIETT

IN A WAY THE IMAGE OF VIDAL SASSOON IS STRONGLY ROOTED IN THE 60S. AND SO IS THE DESIGN OF THIS BOOK. IN A WAY VIDAL SASSOON WAS VERY INFLUENCED BY THE BAUHAUS. AND SO, IN A WAY, IS THIS BOOK.

HERE IS WHY.

WHEN I WENT TO THE ROYAL COLLEGE OF ART IN 1962 TO STUDY GRAPHIC DESIGN, THE FIRST YEAR WAS TAUGHT BY ANTHONY FROSHAUG. HE HAD JUST ARRIVED FRESH FROM TEACHING GRAPHICS AT THE HOCHSCHULE FUR GESTALTUNG AT ULM, IN GERMANY, WHICH WAS THE DIRECT DESCENDANT OF THE THEN-DEFUNCT BAUHAUS. WHAT HE TAUGHT US HAS SINCE HAD A HUGE INFLUENCE ON ALL MY VISUAL THINKING. THIS IS STRANGE BECAUSE, AT THAT TIME, I WAS NOT HAPPY WITH THIS VERY, VERY STRICT COURSE. BUT THIS WAS GOOD BECAUSE, IN MY FRUSTRATION, I USED TO SNEAK DOWN THE CORRIDOR TO THE PAINTING DEPARTMENT WHICH I FELT WAS MUCH MORE ME. I WAS INTO BEAT POETRY AND ALL THINGS POETIC (I.E., NOT THE BAUHAUS). ALTHOUGH I NEVER MADE A MOVE TO THE PAINTING DEPARTMENT, IT WAS THROUGH MY LOVE OF PAINTING THAT I FELL IN LOVE WITH THE POP ART THAT WAS HAP-PENING LITERALLY IN THE NEXT ROOM. THIS WAS WHERE A HUGELY INFLUENTIAL PHENOMENA WAS GROWING—THE VISUAL BACKDROP TO WHAT WAS TO BECOME THE "SWINGING SIXTIES." SO, AS I SAT ON THAT BENCH IN THE R.C.A. HAVING MY MORNING CHEESE ROLL AND CUP OF TEA, TO THE LEFT WAS THE GRAPHIC DESIGN DEPARTMENT AND TO MY RIGHT WAS THE POP ART HAPPENING PAINTING SCHOOL. BOTH WOULD HAVE A VAST INFLUENCE ON EVERYTHING THAT I DID LATER, INCLUDING THE DESIGN OF THIS BOOK. **DESIGN NOTES**

CREDITS

SPECIAL THANKS

A VERY SPECIAL THANKS TO VIDAL'S WIFE, RONNIE, WHOM WE WOULD HAVE BEEN LOST WITHOUT. HER ASSISTANCE IN RESEARCH AND STORYTELLING PROVED INVALUABLE.

JULIAN VOGEL AND MODUS PUBLICITY

JULIA SLOAN

ARCHIVE PRODUCER
TAMSIN RAWADY

LEGAL BY
LISA CALLIF, DONALDSON & CALLIF

VIDAL SASSOON IS JUST THE GREATEST HAIRDRESSER—
HAIR CUTTER—HAIR STYLIST EVER. HE TAUGHT THE WORLD
HOW TO CUT AND STYLE HAIR. HE TAUGHT WOMEN HOW
TO TREAT AND LIVE WITH THEIR HAIRCUT AND TO KEEP IT
IN BRILLIANT, GLOSSY PERFECTION WITH THE HAIR FALLING
BACK INTO SHAPE WITH EVERY TOSS OF THE HEAD. VIDAL
TAUGHT HOW TO FLATTER AND PERFECT THE FACE—THE
EYES, CHEEKBONES AND JAW, AND THE HEAD ALTOGETHER.

VIDAL SASSOON LIBERATED WOMEN FROM HOURS SPENT
SITTING BOILED UNDER A BONNET HAIR DRYER WITH METAL
ROLLERS SKEWERED TO THEIR SCALP WHILE THEIR HAIR
DRIED. THIS TORTURE HAD TO TAKE PLACE AT LEAST ONCE A
WEEK TO KEEP UP THE OLD LOOK.

MARY QUANT

ART DIRECTION AND DESIGN
STEVE HIETT

DESIGN ASSOCIATE
SARAHMAY WILKINSON

EDITOR
HEATHER GORDON

PRODUCER
JACKIE GILBERT-BAUER

ASSOCIATE DESIGNER / IMAGE COMPILATION AND RESEARCH
GENEVIEVE SHEPPARD

PRODUCTION
THOMAS PAULY

THIS BOOK IS A COMPILATION OF QUOTES AND MEMORIES FROM VIDAL
SASSOON WITH ADDITIONAL QUOTES FROM FRIENDS AND COLLEAGUES.
SUPPLEMENTARY WRITING AND EDITING COMPLETED BY HEATHER GORDON.